New World Disorder

The Decline of U.S. Power

By David Ranney

ISBN: 1493740229

ISBN 13: 9781493740222

Library of Congress Control Number: 2014901746

CreateSpace Independent Publishing Platform, North Charleston, SC

Acknowledgements

A number of people have been very helpful to me as I wrote the book. Several of these people read an earlier version of the manuscript and offered very useful comments. These included Dan Baker, Teresa Cordova, John Garvey, Loren Goldner, Don Hammerquist, Peter Little, Nick Paretsky, Bob Wagner, and Pat Wright. Mari Anderson and Fritz Damler assisted with the editing and have formatted it for publication. Mari Anderson also did the cover design. Pat Wright not only read and commented on the manuscript, she discussed the ideas and concepts with me nearly every day for the past year. She continuously encouraged me to keep at it when I was struggling with the project. Thanks, one and all!

Table Of Contents

Chapter 4

The Self Destruction of the New World Order – 57

Chapter 5

Prospects – 156

Preface and Overview

During the year 2000 I wrote a book called *Global Decisions, Local Collisions: Urban Life in the New World Order*. The book, published in 2003, was a reflection on the past two decades of my work as a community and labor organizer and activist academic. Among my conclusions, was that in the 1970s and 1980s we experienced what I call a *"crisis of value."* In response, the entire capitalist system underwent a radical restructuring which brutally displaced workers from their jobs and homes. Yet the restructured system, named a "New World Order" by President George H. W. Bush, was not sustainable. It was built on a house of cards— actually a house of credit cards. The New World Order was running on the illusion of fictitious capital in the form of bad credit. Today that house of cards is falling. We are once again in a *crisis of value*. I argue in this book that the present *crisis of value* will result either in the replacement of the global capitalist system or a radical restructuring of the system as has happened in the wake of past crises. This is a time of great opportunity for the creation of a world in which the "full and free development of every human being is its ruling principle."

But it is also a time of great peril. The dominant role of the U.S. in the world that has persisted since the mid 1940s, and today's global form of capitalism are being challenged from many quarters. And that challenge is likely to succeed. What will take its place is not clear. In the U.S., all politicians seem intent on holding onto the present American dominated system. I will argue that this will ultimately fail no matter which party comes to power. Proposals from liberal think tanks that include increased government spending, job sharing, transactions taxes, and "best practices" won't work either. Conservatives wish to return to Reagan era "trickle down" programs and massive social program cuts. This approach didn't work for Reagan and it won't work this time either.

The challenge from the left, despite the rise of the "Occupies," is weak and disjointed. Meanwhile there is a rise in right wing challenges to capitalism. The logic of the far right challenge could lead to a new brand of fascism. The following book continues the analysis begun more than a decade ago to explain the falling house of cards and examine a variety of prospects for the future.

If we understand clearly what has happened in the past and what is happening now, we can then make informed choices about the directions we need to go and thus participate in shaping our own future. It is toward that end that I wrote this book. What ends up happening is really up to all of us—the thought and actions we take and don't take. Below is a summary of the key points I will develop in the remainder of the book.

- The crash of 2008-2009 marks the appearance of a *crisis of value* (Chapter 1)

- A *crisis of value* emerges when the claims on the value generated by the entire global capitalist system are greater than the system is capable of producing. (Chapter 1)

- This suggests that what we experienced beginning in 2008 was not simply "the worst recession since the Great Depression" as many politicians love to say, and what is happening today is not a slow recovery or any sort of recovery. We are at the *beginning point* of a much more serious crisis. (Chapter 1)

- *Crises of value* have emerged throughout the history of capitalism and are inherent in the capitalist system itself. (Chapter 1)

- Historically, when such crises have occurred there have been nasty periods of churning and flailing as businesses, governments and people frantically seek a way out of the mess. (Chapter 2)

- In each case, the result has been massive destruction of claims on value and a radical restructuring of the system that has temporarily resolved the crisis. (Chapter 2)

- The last major *crisis of value* emerged in the late 1960s. The period of churning and flailing lasted until the early 1980s. (Chapter 2)

- The churning and flailing from the late 1960s to the early 1980s included the destruction of industry in the U.S. and much of Europe and its relocation to lower wage regions of the world. It also included radical changes in technology and institutions that made the relocation possible. (Chapters 2 and 3)

- A New World Order that has also been referred to as globalization, the Washington consensus, or neoliberalism, took root in the 1980s. (Chapter 3)

- The New World Order included: movement of industrial production to low wage areas of the world, the elimination of government or union restrictions on that movement, and economic policies that favored anti-inflationary strategies even in the face of unemployment. (Chapter 3)

- The New World Order has contributed to the acceleration of environmental degradation. (Chapter 3)

- A key to the functioning of the New World Order is the use of household debt to make up for the loss of wages due to the movement of industry to low wage areas. (Chapter 3)

- Similarly, government debt was used to make up for the loss of tax revenues that resulted from loss of jobs and income as the manufacturing sector in the U.S. and Europe was destroyed. (Chapter 3)

- Debt was also used in low wage areas of the world as a way to penetrate their economies, making them available to corporations from industrialized nations. (Chapter 3)

- Debt was transformed from simply a series of loans, to commodities that could be bought and sold in global financial markets. Turning debt into a commodity made possible the massive increases in global debt. (Chapter 3)

- The contradictions in the New World Order system have generated a new *crisis of value* that we face today. (Chapter 3)

- By running much of the New World Order on debt made possible by buying and selling that debt, the system has created what I call *phantasms*. These phantom markets for debt have become increasingly removed from any real products, yet they impact prices people pay for real goods and services, including food and housing. (Chapter 4)

- Phantasms generate money for a few but are ultimately not sustainable, as the housing market crash demonstrated. Yet at the same time these markets are essential for the New World Order to continue. In this sense the creation and functioning of New World Order markets contribute to the self-destruction of the New World Order. (Chapter 4)

- The fundamental role of governments in any system is to protect the system it governs. (Chapter 4)

- The economic, military and foreign policies of governments today are designed to protect the New World Order. (Chapter 4)

- Because it promotes and protects policies that are deepening the present *crisis of value*, governments are actually contributing to the crisis and to the ongoing self-destruction of the New World Order. (Chapter 4)

- It is quite possible that the global churning and flailing we are experiencing will continue for some time. This includes uprisings and civil wars, bickering between conservative and liberal politicians over equally untenable policies and programs, an ongoing fiscal crisis, further environmental degradation, and in the U.S., a state of permanent war and the evolution of an increasingly intrusive "national security state." (Chapter 5)

- As part of global churning and flailing we are also seeing various challenges to U.S. leadership of the New World Order. The most serious of these and the most likely to be successful is the effort to destroy the status of the dollar as the global reserve currency. If successful, the loss of the dollar's supremacy will have profound and negative impacts on the ability of the U.S. to use debt to make up for its lack of value production. (Chapter 5)

- There is also the possibility that a radical restructuring will evolve that replaces many of the essential features of the New World Order while maintaining capitalism. One possibility that is currently underway is the seizure of lands and forests that currently support subsistence farming, and the use of that land to build dams, roads, pipelines and factories that employ former agricultural workers at very low wages. Some have called this "extractative" development or "primitive accumulation," and it is being implemented on a significant scale in Asia, Africa and South America. (Chapter 5)

- There is also a possibility for a 21st century fascism to emerge that could be either another form of capitalism or a system in opposition to capitalism. Currently, there are popular fascist movements and examples of fascism in embryo around the world. (Chapter 5)

- There are also possibilities that successful anti-capitalist revolutions will offer a positive alternative to both capitalism and fascism. (Chapter 5)

- These alternatives include: abolishing the law of value, designing a system to meet human needs, and setting goals to create a world where the ruling principle is "the full and free development of every human being." (Chapter 5)

Breaking the "Mind-Forged Manacles"

Before continuing, I want to make a crucial introductory point. Discussions of politics, economics and how to move forward are being hampered by assuming that the system we see before us is the best we can do. We assume that most features of our current system are permanent, and we assess prospects for change using that assumption. Normally, we live our lives assuming that many of its features are permanent. This gives us a starting point for everything we do. It includes some agreed upon boundaries for both thought and action. Living within these boundaries defines a practical, pragmatic life, but the assumption that these boundaries are permanent limits our ideas of what is possible. There are times when it becomes necessary to move beyond those boundaries.

I'm asking you to put on hold all of life's "permanencies," including your concept of human nature. Forget about what is currently permitted and what is not. Forget about what will get this candidate or another elected. Forget about the rules of Congress. Forget about the political power of the banks and the military power of the U.S. Forget about our estimates of what is practical and what is not. Open your mind to *all* possibilities. Only then can you go back to see which of the "permanent" aspects of your life make sense and which do not.

Way back in 1794, British poet William Blake coined the term "mind-forged manacles" to depict the self-imposed limits on thought that hold back human progress.

> I wander thro' each charter'd street,
> Near where the charter'd Thames does flow.
> And mark in every face I meet
> Marks of weakness, marks of woe.
> In every cry of every Man,
> In every Infant's cry of fear,
> In every voice, in every ban,
> The mind-forg'd manacles I hear.

This image of the limitations imposed by "mind-forged manacles" is good to keep in front of us as we seek a way forward out of today's mess.

Some Notes on Reading This Book

This book aims to promote discussion of today's issues in a new way. In order to improve readability, I have not loaded the text with footnotes. In addition, I have avoided debating the many points of view on topics I write about. Instead, I've put a few key terms into italics, defined them immediately then repeated those definitions in a glossary at the end of the text. Secondly, when there are some key references for ideas I put forward or factual material I draw upon, I put the references in parentheses right in the text. At the end of the book I also provide an alphabetical list of key sources. Thirdly, I italicized and made bold those sentences I consider key so you can quickly scroll through each chapter and pick out particularly important points and concepts. The most fundamental points I make are also outlined in the bullet points above, with chapter references, so you can refer back and see what I'm getting at in each chapter. Finally, there are some study questions at the end of each chapter to facilitate discussion of the book.

The book is designed so that each chapter is a building block for the chapters that follow:

- Chapter 1 defines *crisis of value* as the theoretical basis for understanding the particular crisis we face today.
- Chapter 2 shows this theory in action by placing it in a historical context.

- Chapter 3 focuses on how the last *crisis of value* gave rise to the system we currently live under—The New World Order.
- Chapter 4 takes that system and shows the nature of today's *crisis of value*—how the New World Order has become a new world *dis*order.
- Chapter 5 demonstrates how a variety of possible futures could evolve out of that disorder.

You may find some parts of the book easier to read than other parts. Some parts may be of greater interest than others. In spite of the book's logical structure, it is also written so that its parts are self-contained. Feel free to skip over a troublesome part or some of the detailed examples, then come back later to what you missed. The book is also designed to be read by book clubs and study groups. Various people can take a lead in discussing different chapters, using the study questions for that discussion.

Chapter 1

How Our System Works
(And Sometimes Doesn't)

In 2008, the U.S. and Europe experienced a financial crash that was described as the worst recession since the Great Depression. We are still suffering from the aftermath of that crash. People have lost jobs, homes and families. As I will discuss later, I don't think that the terms recession or even depression begin to describe what has happened and is still happening to us.

I contend that the traditional measures used to counter a business recession—government spending and tax cuts—are not sufficient to turn things around. The popular idea (with elites) of combining debt relief with austerity will likely make things even worse. Cracking down on greed or putting greedy crooks in jail won't do the trick either, though that might be enormously satisfying. The problems we face do not stem strictly from greed or big corrupt government. They go much deeper. My argument begins by understanding how our economic/political system actually works (or doesn't). At the root of my argument is the notion of economic and political crisis, which I define in this chapter.

There are many theories and conceptions of crisis. Since my objective in writing this book is to provoke thought and discussion rather than try to convince people that my theory makes the most sense (although I believe it does), I am not going to spend much time trying to debate other theories. Rather, I am going to lay out the logic of my own ideas about crisis and let that logic speak for itself. Throughout the book, I use a theory of crisis that I call a *crisis of value*. I believe that such crises are an inherent feature of capitalism, and that the U.S. and the entire world are now in the beginning stages of one.

A summary definition of a *crisis of value* is this: Capitalism has an inherent tendency to produce greater claims on the value generated by the global capitalist system than the system is capable of generating, given the state of technology and production know-how. When this happens, profit rates begin to fall and the system is no longer able to reproduce itself or the people who participate in it. What follows is a period of crisis that includes widespread unemployment, declining living standards, social upheaval and even war. Various actions on the part of ordinary people, the owners of capitalist enterprise, and the governments that are dedicated to keeping the system intact enter a period of *churning and flailing* as they attempt to find a way out the crisis.

Crisis of value includes two key concepts that are important to understand: *capitalism* and *value*. As you will see, I define these concepts differently than our common sense understanding. Most people equate *capitalism* with private markets and label economies with a relatively large public sector as "socialist." This is *not* the way I use the terms *capitalism* or *socialism*. The largest capitalist nations today vary considerably in the relative importance of private markets. Despite all the political banter about "big government," U.S. private enterprise accounts for about 77% of the entire economy. Relative to other nations, this is a large portion. Among European nations, Germany is closest to the U.S. at 72%. Sweden is 68%, England 58%, and France 55%. (These figures are calculated using World Bank statistics on Gross Domestic Product.) It is possible to function as a capitalist system without any private enterprise at all. The former Soviet Union was, in my opinion, a type of *capitalism* called *state capitalism*. So what do I mean by the term *capitalism*? And what is it that makes capitalism…*capitalism*?

What is unique about a capitalist system is the nature of *value* and the way *value* is created and distributed. The secret to the workings of the capitalist system is that workers produce more *value* (which I'll define in a moment) than they get back in the form of wages and salaries. Business owners accumulate some of the value produced by their workers. They use it to meet their own needs and to invest in their businesses in order to keep the system and their businesses going and growing. They play a vital role in reproducing the system. Reproducing the capitalist system includes investing in technology and equipment that workers use to produce value. But in a capitalist economy *everyone* needs to get some of the value produced by workers whether they directly produce this value or not. Everyone living in a capitalist system needs some of the value generated by the system in order to live a decent life and reproduce the next generation. The very survival of the capitalist system depends it.

So what is value? Common sense and Economics 101 courses equate *value* with money and use the prices of goods and services produced by the capitalist system as a measure of their value. This is *not* the way I use the term value. I define *value* in a capitalist system as the necessary labor time needed to produce a good or a service. A *labor theory of value* is an old idea going back to classical economists like Adam Smith, David Ricardo, and Karl Marx. This is still an important theory for today.

Consider this: In my book *Global Decisions, Local Collisions*, I related a conversation I had with two friends back in 2000. We were in a remote area of rural Wisconsin. Year-round residents of this community who were not retirees depended economically on the spending of summer residents from places like Chicago, Milwaukee and Minneapolis, as well as tourists. In the year 2000, an increase of summer residents who had easy access to home loans pushed up the prices of housing and land (real estate). These properties were increasing in their *assessed value*, which is the basis of taxes on houses and land. So property taxes were increasing. One day, I remarked to my friends that land and houses were priced way beyond what they were worth. "What do you mean?" exclaimed one friend, a summer resident from Chicago. "Houses and land are worth whatever people want to pay for them!" A second friend, who was a full time resident on a limited and fixed income replied, "That may be, but if prices and taxes keep going up, people like me won't be able to afford to live here."

1. Value

So what is the *value* of the real estate we were talking about? In a capitalist system a house (excluding the land it sits on), is really two things. On one hand, it is a home that offers shelter, protection from the elements and a safe place to raise a family. This is its *use value*. But in a capitalist system, a house is also considered to be an asset or an investment that is worth money.

This is its *exchange value*. When prices go up so that some people are no longer able to live in their home, *use value* is in conflict with or contradictory to *exchange value*.

However, as my friend pointed out, in a capitalist system, how much a house or anything else is worth at any point in time is determined by its money price. As long as summer residents come to my community and want to buy or build houses, and there are more buyers than houses, prices go up. And they will go up even if that means that long term residents who may be land rich and cash poor are forced to sell and go elsewhere. In a capitalist system, the *exchange value* of everything takes priority over all other considerations, including the house as a home. *Exchange value* is always a higher priority than *use value*.

As we know, eight years after the three of us had that conversation, prices for housing in the U.S. and other parts of the world collapsed. As a result, real estate prices fell drastically in my Wisconsin community. Those who had built or bought summer homes now needed to sell them due to the changed economic conditions. Not only was it hard to find buyers, when they *were* found they expected greatly reduced prices. In cities across the country thousands of people had taken out loans to buy homes when prices were high. When prices fell, they found they owed more than the house was "worth." And, if they lost a job, they couldn't pay off the loan anyway and were either evicted or forced to abandon their homes.

So what, in these examples, was the *value* of the real estate? Was it its price in 2000? Was it its price in 2009? What is the *value* of anything, for that matter? As I noted earlier, common sense and Economics 101 classes treat money prices as if they are the same as value. According to this view, prices are determined partly by people bidding in markets based on their income and how badly they want the product or service they're trying to buy (the demand). Prices, in the conventional view, are also based on how much factory owners or builders are willing to sell in the market at various prices based on their costs (the supply). But from the recent rise and fall of housing prices, we've learned that prices can be "too high" or "too low." So the question becomes: what is the relationship of *value* to money price? I believe the answer to this question is fundamental to understanding *capitalism* and the nature of the present crisis we face.

There is logic behind the idea that the value of all goods and services is determined by the labor time required to produce them. All goods and services are produced by labor. Some require more labor time than others. The amount of labor time that goes into producing a house is far greater than the labor time spent producing a pair of shoes. This difference may or may not be reflected in their prices. But this is why a house has more *value* than a pair of shoes even though both are essential to meet basic human needs. (Note that in order to clarify the concept of value, I am considering here only the house—the value of the land it sits on is a more complex matter. Also, I compare a house to a pair of shoes because both meet fundamental human needs and thus have similar use values yet different prices that reflect exchange values.)

The *labor theory of value* helps explain why there is a contradiction inherent in the capitalist system itself. Competition among individual capitalists requires individual business owners and the system as a whole to lower costs for each item produced each day or each hour. This is done in a variety of ways:

- investing in labor-saving machinery
- moving production to places where business owners can get a higher share of the value produced by paying lower wages
- offering fewer benefits, or making workers work faster and longer

2. Crisis

However, since the value of goods and services is the labor time required to produce them, many of these measures actually lower the value of what is being produced. Meanwhile, it is important to understand that even when someone is unemployed or being paid below the cost of living and reproducing, they still have the same basic needs. They still need a home and shoes as well as food, health care and education. Put another way, the use value and need for these things remains the same. People all over the world therefore have a *claim on the value* generated by the system as a whole no matter what their economic circumstances are. If basic human needs are not met, the system can't continue because people simply can't reproduce themselves.

There are other kinds of claims on value, which also explain the basic contradiction in the capitalist system that generates *crises of value*. As capitalists invest in technology and equipment to increase the production of value, they need the participation of a variety of businesses that don't produce value themselves. These businesses have a claim on value without producing value and that claim eventually becomes greater than the value generated by the new technology and equipment.

These businesses include the so-called FIRE industries: finance, insurance and real estate, and legal services. Stock and bondholders also have a claim on value. The purchase of a stock or bond enables corporations to meet expenses, purchase new machinery or make other investments in their businesses before value is even created. This gives the purchaser of the stocks and bonds a claim on future values—values that haven't even been created yet.

There are also social claims on value that include environmental cleanup, and social services like Medicare, Social Security, Medicaid, Food Stamps and public housing, which maintain a basic standard of living for those who are unable to work or unable to find work. There are public claims on value for public health and safety (police and fire). And there are claims generated by the cost of military forces and weapons. Claims on value by government include services required to manage the capitalist system as a whole, such as printing and managing the supply of money, economic policy and government regulation of business. (See Chapter 4 for an in-depth discussion of government services.)

As economic development in a capitalist system proceeds, basic human needs, the needs of business and the population for services, and the drive to reduce costs tend to reach a state where claims on value exceed the amount of value the system as a whole can generate. This is a *crisis of value*.

During a crisis, the conflict between all of these claims and the need to accumulate surplus value becomes very great. Profit rates begin to fall. They fall because the capacity of the system to produce value is not adequate to meet the growing claims on value. For the capitalist system, the only way out of this is to destroy some of these claims and change the way capitalism functions.

3. Churning and Flailing

As I write this, some destruction of claims on value is underway. When private corporations cancel or reduce pension payouts it is an example of the destruction of claims on value. State public employees are seeing some of their pension benefits cut. The entire City of Detroit is filing for bankruptcy. This will mean that pensions of city workers, including police and firemen, will be cut. City workers will be laid off and the residents of Detroit will experience many reduced or eliminated public services.

Historically, there have been a number of lengthy periods of *crises of value*. During these periods, there has been immense destruction of claims on value through wars that physically destroy value-producing factories and human lives. The destruction of claims on value also occurs with business closings, disinvestment and other means that I will explore in this book.

During crises of value, there have been severe recessions, when the economy ceases to grow. As profit rates fall, unemployment rises and wages stagnate. Businesses collapse or relocate, creating human misery and civil unrest within nations. And since the crises have not been confined to single nations, tensions between nations and among national blocs have increased as each nation-state attempts to recover at the expense of others. The result has been war. Both war and sharp economic downturns destroy claims on value and create the basis for a temporary resolution to the crisis. But all this *churning and flailing* exacts a heavy burden on ordinary people. Lives are lost, homes and property taken or destroyed, living standards are demolished and masses of people displaced.

The conflict each period has generated has raised the question of whether the outcome of each crisis will be a radically restructured form of capitalism, or something else. In past crises, destruction of some claims on value and a radical restructuring of the system have *temporarily* resolved the crisis. While this temporary solution allowed the system to grow and brought relief and even prosperity to some, the contradictions remained. And those contradictions generated new crises with all the attendant churning and flailing: war, destruction of claims on value and destruction of human lives. Since we are presently living with yet another crisis of value, the question of a direction forward is on the table. We all have an opportunity to help shape the outcome.

Discussion Questions

1. What does the author mean when he says that what is unique about capitalism "is the nature of value and the way value is distributed"?
2. What, according to the author, is value? How does that correspond with the way you tend to view value?
3. What does the author mean by a *crisis of value*?
4. On what basis does the author contend that crises of value are inherent in the capitalist system? Do you agree?
5. What is the significance of the concept of *churning and flailing?*

Chapter 2
Crises Past

There have been three periods of crisis in the last hundred years. The first lasted thirty years, from about 1914 to 1945. The second lasted more than twenty years, running from the late 1960s into the 1980s. Both of these included significant destruction of claims on value and a radical restructuring of global capitalism. The present crisis is a result of the contradictions generated by the temporary resolutions to past crises. The resolution to the crisis of 1914-45 generated the crisis of 1960-80. The resolution of the 1960-80 crisis produced the system we live in today and gave rise to the crisis that we are now facing. For these reasons, our search for a direction forward needs to be informed by an understanding of the past.

1. Crisis and Restructuring: 1914-45

During its first hundred years, the global capitalist system was very unstable with continuous ups and downs. Yet it wasn't until July 28, 1914, that we began to experience massive destruction of many claims on value. That date marked the beginning of World War I, which continued until 1918. Following WWI, the industrial capitalist world experienced the wholesale liquidation of many businesses during the Great Depression in 1929. As the effects of the Depression lingered, another world war began in 1939 and lasted until 1945. The destruction of both capital and human lives during that period was enormous. But it was that destruction that reduced claims on value and allowed a failing capitalist system to restructure and start anew.

Until World War II, England was the most powerful nation in the world. Its vast colonies generated a great amount of value for its capitalists, and to a lesser extent its workers, making it the center of global capitalism. Colonies predated capitalism. They served to facilitate and control trade, including the slave trade. England controlled huge areas in Africa, Asia and the Americas. There were other competing nations in Europe—France, Germany, Spain, Belgium, Portugal—that also had substantial colonial holdings. Turkey controlled much of Eastern Europe, the region that today is known as the Middle East, and Northern Africa. Turkey's colonies were known as the Ottoman Empire.

As capitalism replaced mercantilism (economies based on trade), the role of colonies changed. European nations, and increasingly the U.S., extracted resources from their colonial lands and used them to produce goods at home. The colonies then served as markets for the finished goods. As a *crisis of value* marked by falling profit rates began, the various empires contended with each other for control of colonies. This, in part, was the basis for World War I that began the long process of destroying value production and the claims on it, beginning in 1914.

In the wake of World War I, the colonial domination of the Ottoman Empire was destroyed and carved up among the victorious powers. In addition to Turkey, Germany was also a big loser. England came out on top; the U.S. was not yet a major player. But the crisis of value continued after World War I. It next appeared as the Great Depression in 1929. The Depression destroyed more claims on value. Germany, along with Italy and Spain, once again attempted to recoup their losses. Japan tried to do the same in large parts of Asia, and this led to World War II.

The ongoing *crisis of value*, technological changes in the production process, labor revolt around the globe and world war were part of the churning and instability that have historically accompanied crises of value. They resulted in a major shift in the nature of global capitalism that destroyed prevailing claims on value, moved the center of economic power to the U.S. and its capitalist enterprises, and altered the nature of politics in the U.S. and around the world.

In the early 1900s, Henry Ford's innovations in the production of the automobile ushered in the assembly line. The concept and technique of mass production that evolved was thus termed Fordism. Fordism advanced by bringing more and more parts of the production process under one roof. For example, Ford Rouge, a massive industrial complex in Detroit, produced automobiles in a process that also included the production of steel, glass and much of what went into automobiles and trucks.

A few years later, further innovation introduced "scientific management" to manufacturing. These techniques were known as Taylorism after its founder Frederick Taylor. Taylorism examined every movement each worker made in the production process, measured the time these movements took, and devised more efficient movements that would increase productivity. The combination of Fordism and Taylorism literally turned workers into parts of a huge industrial machine, thus diminishing worker control over the production process while increasing the surplus that could be extracted from the value produced by labor. Since they lowered unit costs, Fordism and Taylorism spread from the U.S. to Europe, but these developments were greatly muted by the Great Depression in 1929.

The combination of crisis and the beginnings of the shift to the Fordist era also gave rise to militant unionism in the U.S. and many other parts of the world. As early as 1905 in the U.S., the Industrial Workers of the World (IWW) began to organize workers in entire industries rather than along craft lines. By organizing on industry lines, the IWW was the first labor organization to begin adapting to the emergence of mass production, where skilled workers and laborers worked side by side. Industrial unionism essentially encouraged class unity, allowing the IWW to pose a vision of "one big union" as an alternative to capitalism itself.

Industrialists and the government fiercely resisted the IWW. Many key IWW leaders were assassinated. The remaining leadership was imprisoned for their opposition to WWI, after they declared: "Capitalists of America, we will fight against you not for you." (*Industrial Worker*, 1917.) Government repression and internal divisions over strategy effectively destroyed the organization. But in the aftermath of the Great Depression, another militant industrial union movement emerged: the Congress of Industrial Organizations (CIO). Their break from the more moderate American Federation of Labor (AFL), which continued to organize their members by craft rather than industry, was preceded by a series of often violent strikes. President

Roosevelt attempted to secure labor peace by instituting new legislation that affirmed the right of workers to organize, form unions and bargain collectively. Employers' refusal to recognize these rights generated continued militant strikes that at times included the occupation of factories, challenging the permanence of the factory as private property.

It wasn't until World War II that both economic crisis and labor militancy dissipated. The latter was due to the fact that most workers supported the war effort, participating either as soldiers or on the factory floor. By the summer of 1944, the war was winding down. In July, a conference attended by the representatives of 44 nations in Bretton Woods, New Hampshire, mapped out a strategy for post-war development. The U.S. was in a position both economically and politically to determine the terms of this strategy; both its industry and infrastructure were intact. The other nations of Europe were in shambles. The destruction of factories, homes, economic institutions and human lives all over the world amounted to a massive destruction of value. The Bretton Woods Agreement became the basis for reorganizing the global capitalist system. It was designed to rebuild Europe and Japan on U.S. terms, and endured until the early 1970s.

A key provision of Bretton Woods was that the U.S. dollar became the international "reserve currency," which meant that the dollar was used to settle all international financial transactions. Its value was fixed relative to the currencies of other nations and backed by gold. Essentially, this made the U.S. dollar "as good as gold." Bretton Woods also established institutions—International Monetary Fund [IMF], World Bank, the General Agreement on Tariffs and Trade [GATT])—to facilitate this system.

The IMF and the World Bank had well-defined roles in the rebuilding of Western Europe. The IMF's purpose was to maintain stable values for currencies to facilitate international trade. If shortages and development bottlenecks caused inflationary pressures, the IMF would provide short-term loans and technical assistance to resolve the problem. The World Bank was established as a financial intermediary between U.S. lenders and the countries of Europe who needed dollars to buy exports and engage in long-term development projects. The funding of these two institutions came from member nations; voting rights on IMF and World Bank policy were based on the size of each nation's financial stake. This arrangement enabled the U.S. to maintain political and economic control over international development policy.

The General Agreement on Tariffs and Trade (GATT) was established to facilitate trade among nations by preventing costly trade wars. Most nations charged a tax on the products of other nations, called tariffs. If a particular tariff was set too high, another nation could raise tariffs on other products. A general rise in tariffs could threaten trade all together. And since most nations needed products from other nations, such a trade war could hinder economic development.

Historically, most of the developed nations of the world used selective tariffs to protect their key industries from competition until they could get established. The trick had always been how to keep that process from turning into an all out destructive trade war. Negotiating tariffs between nations could be used to maintain a "managed trade" system. The GATT was established to do that among its twelve original member nations. Member nations would meet to establish a general set of principles that were to be the basis for bilateral trade agreements between GATT members.

The lending activities of the IMF and World Bank, the trade arrangements of the GATT and the establishment of the dollar as the international reserve currency enabled U.S. corporations to expand their profitability and blunt the effects of cyclical crisis. The Bretton Woods Agreement had as its U.S. domestic counterpart, government fiscal and monetary policies that used government powers to spend, tax, print money, and establish the terms of borrowing and extending credit. These powers were used to stimulate economic growth. Post World War II development within the industrial nations of the world consolidated Fordism and Taylorism as the global method of production. Productivity growth (the amount each worker produced in a certain amount of time) was thus on the rise.

All of these post World War II developments under the aegis of the Bretton Woods Agreement made the U.S. the dominant power in the capitalist world. All rivals had been greatly weakened by the war. Germany, Italy, Spain, and Japan lost their colonies during and immediately after the war. Moreover, the end of World War II also sparked a resurgence of anti-colonial movements that particularly weakened England and France. India, including what is today Pakistan and Bangladesh, Jordan, Palestine (which later became Israel), Egypt, Burma and Ceylon became independent of England. France lost Lebanon, Syria, Laos, Cambodia and eventually Vietnam, Algeria, Tunisia and Morocco.

The Philippines declared independence from the U.S. during this period, but the U.S. was not greatly affected by postwar anti-colonial movements. In fact, the U.S. began to implement neocolonial policies, using economic and military aid to dominate newly independent governments and achieve the same objectives as past colonial administrations.

Initially, organized labor in the U.S. attempted to use to its advantage postwar prosperity and favorable labor legislation won during clashes prior to the war. Militancy returned to the U.S. in the early years of postwar development, but it was short lived. The U.S. dominant role in postwar economic growth enabled U.S. capitalists to generate a great amount of surplus value. Some of this surplus was offered to U.S. labor leaders in exchange for labor peace. As a result, union leaders generally decided to accommodate their objectives to the new Fordist era.

The accommodation began with a strategic decision on the part of the United Auto Workers (UAW), a key CIO union, to tie the fortunes of its workers to increasing productivity. UAW's contract with General Motors in 1946 was a critical step for the U.S. labor movement. In that contract, the UAW agreed to maintain labor peace for a period of three years in return for a share of UAW's growing, productivity-based profits. The problem with the UAW-GM contract, which became a model for CIO union negotiations, was that it ceded to management the terms of productivity growth.

This would come back to haunt the labor movement in the future. The union guarantee of labor peace undermined the militancy that had been the basis for labor's gains in the past. That militancy had challenged the methods used by capitalists to accumulate surplus values. Taylorism, automation, and speeding up assembly lines had increased worker productivity but diminished labor's control over the conditions of their own work.

It reduced each worker to an appendage of the giant machine called the assembly line. The prewar labor militancy directly challenged this, using slow-downs, strikes and factory occupations. But postwar, higher wages were exchanged for labor peace and the long-term contract, effectively taking off the table the militant labor challenge to the production process.

This accommodation by the labor unions emboldened big business to make a move on the legislative front. In 1947, the National Association of Manufacturers (NAM) drafted a legislative assault on the terms of the Wagner Act, considered by many workers to be a "bill of rights." The resulting Taft-Hartley Act reinstituted injunctions, outlawed mass picketing and secondary boycotts, and facilitated lawsuits against unions. It became a serious setback for labor and the union movement. Taft-Hartley merely institutionalized the postwar deal between management and labor. It was a bitter pill, swallowed not only by the unions but by the bulk of their members, as the cost of a greater share of the profits that came to post World War II America.

U.S. unions also agreed to support the government's Cold War era foreign policies. While the U.S. emerged from World War II as the dominant capitalist nation, the Soviet Union began to compete for spheres of influence in the newly independent developing nations throughout the world. This competition for resources touched off the Cold War. Cold War politics began to dominate U.S. domestic politics. Since the struggle with the Soviet Union was labeled as a struggle between communism and capitalism, union leaders came under considerable pressure to get rid of "communists" in their unions. They were also required to lend material support to U.S. efforts to undermine "communist influences" abroad.

In 1948, the CIO leadership passed a resolution that required affiliated unions to support politicians and policies of the United States favored by the CIO Executive Council. In 1949, those unions that did not comply were labeled subversive and expelled. As a result, many unions expelled leaders who would not comply.

In 1955, the CIO merged with the AFL creating the AFL-CIO. In the 1960s, the AFL-CIO cooperated with the U.S. Central Intelligence Agency (CIA) in overseas operations that were designed to both export their model of "business unionism" abroad and to participate in destabilizing governments or unions that opposed U.S. foreign policy. Three offices were established within the AFL-CIO for this purpose: the American Institute for Free Labor Development (AIFLD), which operated in Central and Latin America, the African American Labor Center in Africa, and the Asian American Free Labor Institute in Asia.

The Fordist period in the U.S. benefited a broad spectrum of the population. World War II, the process of rebuilding Europe after the war, and the ability of U.S. corporations to extract natural resources from recently independent nations of the developing world brought great economic power to the U.S. The terms of the accommodation with labor meant that labor, including both those who were and those who were not producing value, gained a greater share of the *real income* (what wages could buy) derived from U.S. dominance of the global economy. The distribution of income during this period was far more equal than it is today. Also, commodities were sold at lower prices. As real incomes rose, many workers were able to buy cars, homes and appliances and move into newly developing suburbs. But there were contradictions.

One contradiction for U.S. workers within the Bretton Woods/Fordist system was that not all workers enjoyed its benefits. As a result, a major civil rights movement began in the mid-1950s, and exploded in the 1960s and into the early 1970s. Civil rights struggles that began with efforts by blacks to achieve voting rights and the right to use public facilities in the South, grew to include struggles to desegregate all white neighborhoods in the North. The movement also gained momentum in labor unions, where discrimination was rampant.

In the 1960s, separate shop caucuses were formed in many workplaces to push the demands of black, Latino and women workers. In addition, many workers began to resist the increasing pace of work generated by the extension of Fordist production into automation. Throughout the 1950s there were waves of wildcat strikes in mining, auto and steel industries. Black worker caucuses led many of these strikes. Union leaders, facing injunctions and severe sanctions under Taft-Hartley, joined management to try to suppress both civil rights activities and the struggles against automation that the caucuses had championed. As a result many of the industrial unions became badly divided.

2. Crisis and Restructuring: 1960s – 1980s

By the late 1960s, the postwar demand that drove U.S.-centered prosperity was beginning to diminish as rebuilding was completed in Europe and Japan. In addition, labor struggles were increasing labor's share of the value they were producing. U.S. civil rights struggles began to achieve some measure of success leading to greater wage equality among white men, people of color and women. Thirdly, former colonies began to resist U.S. domination by waging a series of anti-imperialist struggles around the world.

The U.S. had been intervening covertly, or with military advisors and financial aid, in the developing world's liberation struggles. However, between 1965 and 1975, the U.S. became bogged down in a "dirty little war" in Vietnam. The war was fueled by fears that the Soviets were gaining spheres of influence around the world by backing insurgents in the anti-imperialist movements. The war weakened the U.S. both economically and politically. Adding to U.S. political setbacks was the growing momentum of the civil rights movement, which ultimately joined the antiwar movement. The political movements also spread to much of Europe as well as many developing nations. Ultimately, the U.S. lost the war in Vietnam in spectacular fashion.

These developments led to a *crisis of value* that was centered in the U.S. The claims on value generated by the Bretton Woods/Fordist system were growing more rapidly than the production of new value. Another period of chaotic churning and flailing began. The first sign of a new *crisis of value* was falling profit rates in the late 1960s.

Falling profit rates appeared in most developed nations but were particularly severe in the U.S. Then, in the early 1970s the U.S. economy, among others, experienced major bouts of inflation. Rising prices meant goods and services were being bought and sold above their value. Also, the U.S. began to run trade deficits (more foreign goods coming into the U.S. than U.S goods going out) and a balance of payments deficit (more money going out than coming in).

The 1943 Bretton Woods Agreement had made the dollar the international reserve currency. Now, because of the deteriorating economic and political conditions in the U.S., other nations in the developed world were forced to adjust their own domestic economic policies to conform to the fluctuating demand for dollars. In some cases that meant keeping both prices and employment low at home. As the U.S. based system was politically and economically weakened both domestically and abroad, other nations began to question the viability of the U.S. economy and dollar's continuing ability to serve as a global reserve currency. As a result, France led some international efforts to cash in dollars for gold.

In 1971, President Nixon initially devalued the dollar then eventually took it off the gold standard. Then in 1973, he declared that the value of the dollar would be allowed to float based on market demand. Since a fixed value for the dollar backed by gold was at the heart of the Bretton Woods system, that act constituted a cancellation of the Bretton Woods Agreement. It essentially brought a formal end to the system put into place at the end of World War II. The scene was now set for a period of deep social, political and economic conflict, which could either completely destroy capitalism or give birth to a radical restructuring of the system. Ultimately, a restructuring was accomplished that maintained the U.S. as the "most powerful nation in the world" and at the center of global capitalism. But this was preceded by more than a decade of chaotic churning and flailing as other nations challenged U.S. domination, and all the leaders of global capitalism sought a way out of the growing crisis.

3. Churning and Flailing

The economies of the developed capitalist world continued to decline. Two "oil shocks" added fuel to the fire. In 1973, a cartel of oil-producing nations based in the Middle East (OPEC) withheld oil production needed by the U.S. and other industrial nations to retaliate for U.S. support of Israel in the Arab-Israeli War. This created oil shortages that drove prices sharply upward. In 1979, there was a second such shock related to the revolution in Iran. Both cases demonstrated that the post-World War II system of surplus value needed an unlimited supply of oil at stable prices. OPEC's actions placed that need in jeopardy. Both shocks caused high levels of inflation. The industrial nations responded by instituting national economic policies—particularly high interest rates—that restricted industrial expansion and led to unemployment. The result was stagflation: simultaneous inflation and unemployment.

As the *crisis of value* accelerated, anti-capitalism began to emerge within the social protest movements and anti-imperialist liberation struggles. The U.S. dominated system, weakened both economically and politically by the crisis, was in jeopardy. Against these trends came a move on the part of global elites—businesses, governments, and academic intellectuals—to generate a radical restructuring of global capitalism itself. In the previous period, two world wars had destroyed claims on value while establishing grounds to move global power to the U.S. Rebuilding after the wars also created a demand for the expansion of production. Postcolonial political conditions enabled the new system to dominate weakened, under-developed nations in order to acquire a reliable flow of cheap resources. And new production technologies based on Fordism and Taylorism were in place and ready to go. But the *crisis of value* that emerged in the late 1960s and early 1970s lacked a basis for the reorganization of capitalism, allowing significant anti-capitalist initiatives to grow.

In response, business leaders, politicians and sympathetic academicians throughout much of the capitalist world began to formulate the outlines of a radical restructuring of capitalism. Forums like the Organization for Economic Cooperation and Development (OECD), the Trilateral Commission and the Bilderberg Group as well as established Bretton Woods Institutions like the International Monetary Fund (IMF) and the World Bank held conferences and produced papers and proposals. They uniformly agreed that the heart of their problem was that labor was getting too great a share of value. As Jacques de Larosiere, Chairman of the International Monetary Fund so bluntly put it:

> "Over the past four years (1980-83)...a clear pattern (has emerged) of substantial and progressive long term decline in rates of return to capital. There may be many reasons for this. But there is no doubt that an important contributing factor is to be found in the significant increase over the past 20 years or so in the share of income being absorbed by employees...This points to the need for a gradual reduction in the rate of increase in real wages over the medium term if we are to restore adequate investment incentives."

A possible model for how to achieve this was waiting in the wings. In 1973, a military coup in Chile, backed by the U.S. Central Intelligence Agency, ousted a popularly elected socialist government. The leader of the junta, Augusto Pinochet, subsequently instituted an economic program promoted by University of Chicago-trained economists and their mentor, Professor Milton Friedman. The Chilean economic program included tight money to end inflation, drastic reductions in government spending, currency devaluation, and the opening of markets for goods and capital to foreign investors.

The Chilean experiment suggested the outlines of a strategy that could destroy claims on value through a process of reducing production costs. A key focus of the strategy was the cost of labor, but other kinds of production costs were also targeted. These included the cost of raw materials and other inputs into the production process, the cost of environmental controls and clean up, and costs associated with the demands for worker and human rights.

Since all of these costs were high in the U.S. and other industrial nations, such a strategy required a massive movement of production to the developing world where wages were low, worker rights and environmental standards were lax to non-existent, and where there was a ready supply of workers who desperately needed jobs. In short, there was a need for capital to become highly mobile. And there was a need to contain the problems that would be generated by a rapid loss of living wage jobs in the U.S. and other industrial nations.

The Chilean economic experiment previewed needed economic policies that were rapidly institutionalized in the form of what became known as the "Washington Consensus" or simply "globalization." They were a combination of new economic policies initiated by Milton Friedman's Chicago trained economists in Chile, and a set of social policy ideas coming from conservative U.S. political thinkers. (More on that later.) For now, it is important to point out that the implementation of these policies on a global scale took nearly a decade. Along the way there were massive dislocations and relocations that exacted a huge human toll. These included job losses, income stagnation and decline, and income redistribution that enriched a small fraction of the population and drove many into poverty. Increased homelessness and mounting household and government debt also began to appear.

Discussion Questions

1. What is the significance of the Bretton Woods Agreement? What were some of its key provisions?
2. What were some key developments that gave rise to a *crisis of value* in the late 1960s and 1970s?
3. What are some of the elements of the *churning and flailing* that appeared between 1960 and 1980?

Chapter 3
Construction of a New World Order

The system we presently live in, what the first President Bush called a "New World Order," was more than a decade in the making. It radically restructured the way in which capital appropriated and distributed surplus value throughout the world. The New World Order was not the result of some grand master plan mapped out by a few individuals. It was not, as some have contended, the outcome of any great conspiracy. The broad goal of lowering labor's share of value by moving production to low wage, low regulation parts of the world was initially posed in a number of papers produced by elite think tanks and institutions like the World Bank and the International Monetary Fund. The approach that was previewed in Pinochet's Chile emerged in fits and starts and was elaborated upon in many different settings. It included a number of different dimensions, as laid out below:

1. Flexible Manufacturing

The goal of reducing labor's share of the surplus value meant, among other things, getting rid of manufacturing jobs in the industrial nations, especially in the U.S. where wages, benefits and work rules generated the highest costs. Flexible manufacturing was a term used to describe a new kind of automation that reduced the number of workers required in the manufacturing process by eliminating the need for large-scale mass production. Flexible manufacturing replaced the mass production or "Fordism" of the previous era. Evolving computer technology was used to enable firms to produce their products, or parts of their products, in small batches with fewer workers. Robots that could perform multiple tasks with different tools were often at the center of the process. Programmed machines included an automated system to get materials to the point of production. This form of production also uses computer-based systems that reduce the need to carry a large inventory of parts or materials, making possible "just in time" delivery as the production continues. These flexible systems also make it possible for a firm to produce a number of different products simultaneously or sequentially.

Flexible manufacturing not only enables production with fewer workers, it also enables firms to outsource parts of the production process to other locations. A prime example of this development is the automobile. There is no longer such a thing as an "American car." Unlike Detroit's Ford Rouge plant (now demolished) that made all the parts of the car, including steel, glass and plastic in one massive location, today's cars have materials and parts from all over the world. Chrysler, for example, initiated a joint venture with Mitsubishi and Hyundai called the Global Engine Manufacturing Alliance. Presently this group has the capacity to turn out two million engines a year in five factories, located in the U.S., Japan and South Korea. The engines share a common basic design, but that design can be adapted to a variety of engine specifications to meet the needs of many different car makes and models.

Flexible manufacturing's characteristics also enable outsourcing and/or joint manufacturing for smaller products. For example, in 2005 I visited the Master Lock factory in Milwaukee. They had outsourced their lock assembly to Mexico while continuing to fabricate the lock parts in Milwaukee. The Mexico operation was subsequently transferred to China where wages were even cheaper. According to employees in Milwaukee, the impetus for these moves was that Walmart, a major outlet for Master Locks, demanded lower wholesale prices. Master Lock responded to this demand by dividing the production process. Fabrication and design of lock parts remained in Milwaukee while the assembly of the locks was exported to extremely low wage nations.

2. Flexible Locations

Flexible manufacturing enabled everything from cars to padlocks to sneakers to be produced anywhere in the world. It also made it possible to break up the production process. Car engines, brakes, windows, transmissions, etc. could be manufactured in a number of different locations and the car could be assembled elsewhere. In part this involved the development of computer-based small batch production. There were also computer software innovations that could set up global supply chains so that pieces of the product would arrive when and where they were needed without the costs of carrying large inventories. In addition, there were transportation innovations that made it all cost-effective. Large containers that could be moved from ship to truck to railroad car, and an infrastructure for loading at "break in bulk" locations to facilitate this movement, were also developed as part of the New World Order.

These transport innovations also made a number of products completely footloose. The NIKE traveling sneaker is a good example. NIKE, with its famous swoosh, became a marketing shell that outsourced the manufacturing of its sneakers, shirts, jackets and equipment to other firms in a variety of locations around the world. The production of its various lines of sneakers, for example, moved a number of times from country to country, wherever labor and other costs were lowest. Mexico, Vietnam, Indonesia and South Korea were all stopping points for the footloose traveling sneaker.

These innovations in the production process and transport generated the development of global supply chains that were initially invisible to workers and their unions. An apparent labor victory in wages and benefits in the U.S. could be wiped out in an instant if the struggle was isolated from labor located at other points in the global supply chain. A labor "victory" in one place could result in management simply moving parts of the production process to other places around the world.

3. Flexible Workers and Deregulation

Another important accomplishment of flexible manufacturing was to rid the system of a variety of government regulations and work rules that not only added to costs but would make flexible manufacturing systems themselves impossible. Moving production or parts of production outside the U.S. and other industrialized nations circumvented government regulations geared to protect the environment and union rules designed to protect worker health, safety, and fairness in job assignments.

Weakened unions were then in no position to enforce prior work rules as new flexible operations opened at home.

During the period prior to World War II, labor militancy had been directed toward working conditions on the shop floor. The upside of unions going to long-term contracts was that "management prerogatives" were greatly curtailed. Job descriptions, the basis for promotions to those jobs, the number of workers required for certain jobs, the scheduling of breaks and many other aspects of work were all subject to collective bargaining. And once the bargain was struck, these conditions of work were put into the contract. Union labor's political strength began to be reflected in government regulations that defined "unfair labor practices." This included measures to protect the health and safety of workers on the job as well as the environmental impacts of manufacturing, such as air and water pollution standards.

But as firms developed the capacity to move production and outsource parts of production, the contradictions in the contract system and the fragility of government regulation became apparent. When factories shut down, union contracts became null and void. The Taft-Hartley Act made significant resistance by organized labor illegal. Moreover, unions had ceded to management the right to determine worker productivity, which made unions part of the system that was attacking its own members. Once the old factories and old contracts were gone, it was possible to open up new factories inside or outside of the U.S. with fewer workers and a system of flexible labor in force.

U.S. corporations led the charge to eliminate work rules at home and institute regimes of flexible production and flexible labor. But in order to implement flexible production on a global scale by moving high wage jobs to low wage nations around the world, they needed to break down political resistance from governments around the world. Unlike the development of flexible production, the development of institutions to open up the economies of low wage nations required action on the part of the governments of the industrial nations. The U.S. Government was able to handle this problem, but it didn't happen overnight.

4. Institutionalizing the New World Order

Part of the framework for the institutionalization of the New World Order began with a massive expansion of loans to developing nations. Former colonies of European nations in Africa, Latin America and around the world had been weakened by years of looting by colonial powers. Some of the new national leaders in the postcolonial world were idealistic and aspired to progress for their people. Others were corrupt and sought to use the new era to enrich themselves. But all faced serious economic problems, and were thus vulnerable to the entreaties of the U.S. and other former colonial powers to open up their economies by borrowing money.

Some loans came from private banks, but the U.S. government greatly expanded its lending after 1970. In addition, two old Bretton Woods institutions that were controlled by the U.S. Government—the International Monetary Fund (IMF) and the World Bank—also began lending money to the developing world. In the decade between 1973 and 1983, debt in developing nations rose from $100 billion to over $900 billion. Between 1977 and 1982, capital flow from developed to developing nations amounted to $30.5 billion a year. Some of these loans were used to build infrastructure that could support manufacturing facilities. Some went to buy influence by lining the pockets of corrupt elites. But increasingly, short-term loans were made by the IMF to pay off loans. (These data were largely drawn from reports of the International Monetary Fund and World Bank. See especially the World Bank annual reports: *World Development Indicators*.)

By 1982, a global regime of high interest rates geared initially to dampen inflation in the U.S. had spread to the developing world. Between 1977 and 1981, interest rates in the U.S. had been pushed up 60%. Dollars began to flow into the U.S. from many parts of the world to take advantage of the high rates of return. That meant some flowed out of the developing world. This, in addition to the drastic drop in exports, meant that the demand for the currencies of the developing world also collapsed, and a devaluation of these currencies ensued.

Currency devaluation in nations dependent on the outside world for many products meant that many things were suddenly very expensive. Inflation began to cut into the purchasing power of the people of these nations. Thus, many developing nations were plunged into deep recession accompanied by high inflation. To make matters worse, these nations were forced to pay higher interest rates on their flexible-rate loans. As a result, the payments on these loans went sky high. So the IMF was called in to bail out the developing nations with short term "bridge loans."

The IMF loans and the earlier loans made by the World Bank, however, came with conditions attached. And these conditions gave lending institutions virtual control over the economies of many developing countries. By extension, this meant it was the U.S. that exerted this control because the U.S. government controlled IMF and World Bank policies. Nations who had fought wars of liberation to gain political liberty now found themselves in economic subjugation.

The loan conditions became a key part of the infrastructure of the New World Order. They enabled large corporations to move manufacturing facilities or operations to places with low wages and a lack of rules and regulations. The loan conditions became known as "Structural Adjustment Programs" or SAPs. They reflected the initial program designed by University of Chicago economists under General Augusto Pinochet's dictatorship in Chile. Generally speaking, the SAPs consisted of two phases. The first took the name proposed by University of Chicago's Professor Milton Friedman: shock therapy. Shock therapy involved currency devaluation, cuts in social spending to balance budgets, an end to government subsidies of agriculture and locally based businesses, and wage suppression. This was followed by a structural adjustment phase that included privatization of government activities, elimination of barriers to foreign investment, elimination of tariffs on imported goods, and the opening of all services to competition.

The IMF and the World Bank were not the only old Bretton Woods institutions to change directions and become a part of the New World Order. The General Agreement on Tariffs and Trade (GATT) had been established in 1946 to reduce tariffs—a tax on foreign goods that is used to protect local businesses from foreign competitors. The initial negotiations involved twelve nations. Seven rounds of negotiations since that time have added members and increased tariff reductions. But negotiations between 1973 and 1979 added forty new members and began to expand the GATT's mission to include prohibitions against "non-tariff barriers" to trade. These eventually included forms of business regulation, like certain environmental standards and worker rights provisions. While another twenty members were added between 1986 and 1994, the GATT itself—an informal association that negotiated tariffs—was replaced by a new formal institution with greatly expanded powers.

The new organization, established in 1995, was called the World Trade Organization (WTO). Among other things, the WTO added agricultural subsidies to the list of non-tariff barriers to trade. The WTO also introduced "trade related intellectual property rights" (TRIPS) which globalized patents on everything from pharmaceuticals to bull sperm. It began charging royalties for traditional medicines used by local small farmers whose fields and cattle had been "infected" by proprietary genetically modified organisms including corn, wheat and livestock reproduction. The negotiations that turned GATT into WTO also created new institutions to handle dispute resolutions. These were extra-judicial tribunals oriented to the needs of global corporations and the governments of industrial nations.

Breaking WTO rules could mean the imposition of tariffs on a nation's exports by other nations. Ultimately these panels became a vehicle for corporations to sue governments over laws that might reduce profits. Nations not part of WTO are left out of much of world commerce, so most want to get in. There are presently 153 member nations with more seeking admission. Ironically, our old Cold War nemesis, Russia, is the most recent nation admitted to the WTO family. And the U.S. continues to be a dominant player politically in WTO policy deliberations.

The WTO has been supplemented by a number of other multilateral and bilateral trade agreements that include even more detailed rules. The path-breaking agreement was the North American Free Trade Agreement (NAFTA), concluded in 1994. The agreement between the U.S., Canada and Mexico specifies many of the rules that were later included in WTO. The three hundred page document was negotiated over a five-year period. Its many innovations include prohibitions against restrictions on capital flows, opening the nation-members to financial services from one another, and specifying the right of private corporations to sue governments if they impose laws that limit profits in their nation. NAFTA has served as a model for the further development of the WTO and for hundreds of other specific trade agreements.

The European Union is also an important part of the New World Order infrastructure that is presently coming apart at the seams. It is a very different model from NAFTA, including a parliament, central bank and a monetary union (Euro). There is a lot to say about it, but since this book focuses on the U.S., and since its development since World War II has a long and detailed history it would take many pages to do it justice. So I will simply assert that the EU's current woes are also an expression of the global *crisis of value* that I have been describing in the U.S. context. And neither austerity nor more deficit spending offers a good direction forward. (I will discuss the potential of the EU in the final chapter of this book.)

The development of an "infrastructure" as a strategy to use the technologies of flexible manufacturing and flexible labor to move all or parts of production to the most "cost-effective" (cheapest) places in the world is now in place. Most nations in the world are subject to the new rules and institutions developed since the late 1970s. The global integration of production had the effect of destroying many of the claims on value that had been made by high-wage workers and government regulation. Its net effect was to greatly reduce costs of production. Yet the New World Order had created a critical contradiction: *People who create value, as well as those taken out of value production altogether, must get back enough of the world's value production to reproduce themselves and the system as a whole. Destroying labor's claims on value means that without a new addition to the New World Order this critical need of the capitalist system will remain unmet.*

5. Debt as Fictitious Capital

"Complicated financial stuff was being dreamed up for the sole purpose of lending money to people who could never repay it." — Michael Lewis, *The Big Short*

That new addition turned out to be something old in a new package. *The system of credit—the terms and availability of loans—was repackaged so that debt could become a commodity that could be bought and sold on global markets.*

There are a few things that are important to understand about debt. The most important is that it has no value, in the sense discussed earlier, in and of itself. When interest and principle on debt are paid off, those payments must come out of value produced somewhere else, either in real time or in the future. So, unless credit in the society as a whole stimulates the production of value, it is unsustainable. In the case of household debt—credit cards, student loans, car loans, home mortgages—the payments need to come out of the value that households generate by working and making useful goods and services. Debt is therefore a claim on the total value produced in a capitalist system. The same is true of corporate debt. From the perspective of a capitalist system, if that debt is used to invest in factories, equipment or other things used to produce useful goods and services, it is acceptable. But it is still a claim on the value the investments generate.

Government debt is a little different. Government goods and services do not produce value. Taxes and fees for government services, irrespective of who pays them, come out of the value produced directly or indirectly by taxpayers. Since government goods and services are financed primarily by taxes, government spending indirectly represents a claim on value.

An important part of the implementation of the New World Order system was to destroy claims on value that had been generated under the previous Bretton Woods/Fordist system. Since part of the strategy involves reducing the share of value that workers get, meaning less income, the "success" of the strategy will mean that tax revenues decline. So the government either has to reduce spending or borrow to make up the difference. Another major wrinkle in this is that military spending, which also must come out of value production, is made necessary by the strategy to locate production in low cost parts of the world where a military presence is needed to protect investments. (I will discuss this in detail later in the book.)

The broader point is that government debt ended up being part of the strategy initiated in the 1970s to save capitalism. That strategy is now in the process of coming apart at the seams as private and government debt rise above the rate of value production necessary to pay it off.

A growing reliance on both private and government debt is now *required* by the global capitalist system. Increasing corporate debt was caused by the need of corporations to invest in "flexible manufacturing" technology and to relocate operations to various locations around the world. Household debt is needed to make up for the loss of buying power caused by the strategy that aimed to lower labor's share of value. Goods and services produced by human labor can't realize their value unless someone purchases them. And as labor's share of the value they produced was reduced, the realization of value was increasingly achieved by borrowing to purchase needed goods and services. Finally, the decline in tax revenues caused by labor's declining share of the value produced worldwide, combined with the rise in military spending, caused a rise in government debt.

Thus the rising debt we are experiencing in the U.S. and throughout the world is both a necessary part of the New World Order strategy to save capitalism and the Achilles heel that now threatens the system. Debt is being used as a substitute for value, but it has no value in and of itself. For *these reasons* debt is a form of "fictitious capital."

6. Debt as a Fictitious Product

One question remains. What could induce lending institutions to lend money to people whose incomes had been diminished by the loss of living wage jobs? Why would lenders offer credit to nations beyond their ability to pay it back? What, in the words of Michael Lewis in his book *The Big Short*, explains why "complicated financial stuff was being dreamed up for the sole purpose of lending money to people who could never repay it"? The answer is that governments, financial institutions and big business generally conspired to create markets for debt itself that made bad loans highly profitable.

A number of innovations by the financial services industry, plus some key government deregulation, made it possible and profitable for financiers and high-income investors to buy and sell debt like any other commodity or product. As the system developed, not only could people buy houses with loans (mortgages) they couldn't possibly pay back, it was also possible to buy those bad mortgages and sell them in what were known as derivatives markets.

Briefly, a derivative is a piece of paper whose price is derived from the price of some underlying asset. A debt in these markets, which has no value in and of itself, is treated as if it does have value. Its trade assigns a price to debt itself as it becomes an "underlying asset" of the piece of paper it represents. The house or the car that was purchased through this debt falls completely out of the picture. It is irrelevant to debt traders whether individuals pay back the debt or not, unless default on loans becomes so widespread that no one will buy the debt and its price collapses, which is what happened in 2008. All sorts of other kinds of debt—credit card debt, auto loans, student loans and loans to government—were also bought and sold in these markets.

The sale and trading of debt became so profitable that financial institutions in the U.S. began to lobby the Federal Government to remove regulations that limited participation in the new "industry." A key piece of Depression-era regulatory legislation was designed to limit the ability of banks to speculate with commercial bank deposits. The Glass-Steagall Act of 1933 included a number of provisions that essentially prohibited commercial banks from engaging in investment activities that could compromise customer bank deposits.

These provisions, however, had been under attack by major banks and financiers from the beginning. A series of court challenges and the search for loopholes greatly compromised Glass-Steagall. Most of these challenges occurred as the New World Order was being put into place. From the late 1970s through the 1990s there were constant challenges. But in 1998, when Citicorp tried to merge with Traveler's Insurance and then with the investment firm Salomon Brothers (which had already merged with another investment powerhouse, Smith-Barney), it hit a snag. The merger of Citicorp-Travelers with Salomon-Smith Barney was declared illegal under Glass-Steagall. Government regulators, however, tentatively approved the merger for five years to try to work out a "solution." As a result, a new firm, Citigroup, was born.

Citigroup's formation led to an all out effort to get rid of Glass-Steagall once and for all. The charge was led not only by Citigroup but by President Clinton's Secretary of Treasury, Robert Rubin. Before coming to head the Department of Treasury, Rubin had for twenty-six years been a major executive with another investment bank leader, Goldman-Sachs. The President and his Secretary of Treasury, aided by two other key Treasury officials, Lawrence Summers and Timothy Geithner, spearheaded an effort to put a full repeal of Glass-Steagall through Congress. In 1999, this effort resulted in the Gramm-Leach-Bliley Act. The distinction between commercial and investment banking was now blurred and the protection of customer deposits diminished.

Rubin, along with his former colleagues at Goldman-Sachs (including the future Secretary of the U.S. Treasury, Henry Paulson) also led an effort to shoot down a proposal that would give government oversight of derivatives trading outside of the established regulated market institutions. Derivatives trading in established exchanges like the Chicago Board of Trade were already subject to government regulations. But there was no regulation of the activities of private firms like Citigroup and Goldman-Sachs. As a move toward regulating such firms began, the passage of the Commodity Futures Modernization Act of 2000 formally exempted them.

The deregulation of derivatives markets, even in today's charged political atmosphere, has been a bipartisan effort in which government officials have been tightly linked to Wall Street. After leaving public office, Robert Rubin was employed as a consultant and advisor by Citigroup. Lawrence Summers succeeded him at the Department of Treasury. Eventually President George W. Bush appointed Henry Paulson to be his Treasury Secretary. Paulson had previously served as assistant to President Nixon's Chief of Staff, John Ehrlichman, from 1972-73. In 1974 he went to Goldman-Sachs and became its Chief Executive Officer (CEO) before coming to the government in 2006. His compensation package in 2005 was reported to be $35 million dollars. In the late 1990s, Paulson played a major role in the deregulation measures described above. Throughout the period that included the Treasury Secretary tenures of Rubin, Summers and Paulson, a key assistant and player in the Treasury Department was Timothy Geithner. Summers served as President Obama's Chief Economic

Advisor and Geithner was appointed as Secretary of Treasury, a position he held until 2013.

As debt markets grew, the contradiction within them began to appear in 2008. To illustrate this contradiction, consider the case of an individual house, excluding for the moment the land it sits on. The house, as I pointed out earlier, has a value based on the labor required to produce it. But the mortgage on that house has no value beyond the payments being made by the homebuyer. When groups of mortgages represented by bonds called derivatives are bought and sold, traders are trading something that has no value. That is why mortgage derivatives are fictitious products. If the mortgage debt is greater than the price of the house and the land it sits on, and the homeowner loses his or her job and can't make payments on the mortgage, the mortgage derivative becomes worthless. That is exactly what happened in 2008 when a variety of derivatives markets collapsed around the world. However, the practice of trading debt derivatives continues. As soon as the finance sector received their bailout money from the government, they resumed many of the practices that led to the collapse. And the financiers periodically come up with new fictitious products that are essentially trading thin air.

7. Some Outcomes

As debts of all sorts were growing in order to establish the New World Order's plan to save capitalism, derivatives markets for that debt also grew. The selling and buying of derivatives has become increasingly dominated by the "too big to fail" financial institutions that in the U.S. were an outcome of the 1990s deregulation. Goldman, Citigroup and all the others, buy and sell debt primarily through "hedge funds" run by managers within these institutions.

Hedge funds can be independent or a part of large financial institutions. They have no government oversight because they were originally a place where rich people could pool their money and engage in outrageous speculation. Initially referred to as a "rich man's mutual fund," they are private investment funds that charge a performance fee based on returns for their members. They once limited participation to very big investors and made highly speculative investments that got returns as high as 50%. Hedge funds have grown dramatically over the past decade and now account for about one third of all equity trades and over half of all derivatives trading. Their investors are not only rich individuals but also large institutional investors, including pension funds, insurance companies and the banks themselves. Many of the funds go bankrupt on a regular basis, but they continue to be dominated by the large financial houses.

Because derivatives could be sold repeatedly for a profit, they became a very important business for banks around the world. As I will discuss in some detail later in this book, packages of debt became increasingly complex and opaque. And derivative prices became increasingly divorced from the selling prices of the underlying assets. Yet they did succeed in increasing the purchasing power of citizens and governments by increasing the levels of household and government debt.

A look at some of the numbers in the U.S. reveals the steady rise in debt since the 1980s. Household debt, including credit cards, student loans, auto loans and other personal loans as a percentage of after tax income, has risen dramatically. In 1975, such debt was about 60% of household income; by 2012 it was over 120%. Government debt followed the same pattern. Government debt as a percentage of Gross Domestic Product (a measure of the U.S. economy) stood at about 25% in 1975. But it has risen steadily since then. It now stands at about 65%.

The increases in debt are a global phenomenon. Debt is universally high and not sustainable. U.S. debt relative to other nations, however, is not particularly high. In terms of *private debt* as a percentage of income, the U.S. is in the middle range, just a bit lower than Canada and slightly higher than Japan and Germany. For *public debt* there were five nations whose government debt as a percentage of Gross Domestic Product was over 100%. Japan's public debt is 198% of their GDP, followed by Greece, Italy, Belgium and Singapore. Germany, France, Canada and Egypt are all over 80%. In the U.S., the figure is 62%. Despite the U.S. public debt not being high by international standards, we do have a problem. But the problem is global and systemic.

I have argued that the evolving system of credit that sustains the New World Order is itself not sustainable unless it can stimulate greater value than the price of repaying the debt. One way to look at sustainability is to think in terms of a "credit structure." This term is a qualitative notion that looks at debt relative to the mechanism through which it can be repaid. Credit structure operates at a number of levels: global, national or even states and cities. It was nicely conceptualized by an economist named Hyman Minsky, who argued that there are three types of credit structures: hedged, speculative and Ponzi.

A hedged structure means that the interest and principal due on a debt can be paid for out of current income. Home mortgages used to be that way before the explosion of a secondary market on "subprime" mortgages. People who pay their credit card bill each month are in a hedged market. People who have modest car loans that are paid out of a regular paycheck are also in a hedged market. A speculative market, however, requires more than a regular paycheck or reliable government revenues.

In a speculative market, Minsky argues, the borrower can pay off interest out of paychecks or current revenues, but other sources of income or revenue must be found to pay off principal. As an individual, that might mean you would have to get a huge raise, sell some assets, or take out another loan to meet these obligations. If you get behind in your mortgage payments, for example, you might have to sell your car or go to some credit institution, which (at a very high price) will give you a loan to consolidate and begin to pay off your debts. Applying that to a national economy or to the international capitalist system, a speculative credit structure means new loans to pay off old ones.

Ponzi finance is another matter. Minsky named this practice after a con man named Charles Ponzi. He would seek out investors and promise them big returns on some phony investment scheme. Since the scheme was fictitious, Ponzi could pay the investors off only if he found a second group of investors who agreed to invest an even larger amount. He then used the second group's "investment" to pay off the first group (after taking a handsome profit for himself). The scam went on until he ran out of shills. In Minsky's notion of a Ponzi credit structure, there is no income or even assets to pay off debt. Its repayment is fully dependent on finding new sources of money.

In my 2003 book, *Global Decisions, Local Collisions,* I concluded that, "The ongoing development of a New World Order has moved the global credit structure to the brink of a Ponzi finance scam." Since the book was published, the massive growth of derivatives markets has moved us further down that road. Many point to Ponzi scams of people like Bernie Madoff and the excesses of financial institutions and their managers as the heart of the problem that brought about the collapse of 2008. But that is not the case. Corruption, deregulation and greed are part and parcel of the contradiction that now confronts the world. On one hand, the institution and ongoing growth of credit was needed to establish the New World Order system, and it is still needed to keep that system going. But on the other hand, the incentives for lenders required creating and selling fictitious "assets" that masked the fact that value production is not sufficient to reproduce the system or the people who live in it. This contradiction is now appearing with the burst of speculative bubbles, one banking fiasco after another, high and persistent unemployment, housing foreclosures and homelessness, war, and global political instability.

Recently, there have been upturns in housing and stock prices in the U.S. Pundits are talking in terms of "recovery." But the contradictions remain. And they will continue to appear not only in the U.S., but also throughout the world. We are deep into a *crisis of value* as the New World Order system continues a process of self-destruction.

8. The Acceleration of Environmental Degradation

Capitalism *by its very nature* tends to degrade the environment. When that degradation threatens the system, public protest can and has caused the government that protects the system as a whole to step in with environmental regulations. These regulations can slow or in some cases stop the degradation process. But the New World Order's reorganization of global capitalism has increased the pace of environmental degradation through a higher level of global production and consumption. The result of what many call "globalization" has been that the growth of pollution and carbon-inducing industrial practices and global consumption levels has overrun the capacity of nature, technology and governmental regulation to clean up the mess.

There are many measures of environmental quality, and nearly all of them suggest that the earth is warming, resources are depleted, and pollution and waste accumulation is on the rise in many parts of the world. The Earth Quality Institute publishes data on twelve separate indicators of practices that put stress on the environment as well as indicators of environmental quality. Measures of environmental stress include the amount of carbon emissions, polar ice melt, global temperatures, grain harvest yields, and fish catches. They also measure trends in fresh water supply (levels of lakes, rivers, and water tables) relative to the draw on these sources. The Institute also keeps track of the use of alternative energy sources—wind power, solar power and bicycle production—and includes population levels and the rate of economic growth in various parts of the world. The data suggest to me an acceleration of environmental degradation that is outstripping measures taken to offset it.

I am not a trained environmental scientist, but I do have concerns about the consequences of our lack of stewardship when it comes to nature. My interest and concerns were peaked by my work with Chicago workers who were displaced by factory closings in the 1980s and 1990s, and my subsequent activism around the North American Free Trade Agreement (NAFTA) and the World Trade Organization (WTO), that I felt were likely to contribute to more displacement. In questioning the wisdom, and eventually opposing both NAFTA and WTO, I worked closely with organizations and individuals from the U.S. and a number of different nations. We focused our attention on labor rights and the environmental consequences of what came to be known as "free trade," or the Washington Consensus. We tracked a number of firms that had left Chicago and moved operations to Mexico. These firms were subjecting workers to dreadful working conditions, low pay and were simply dumping toxic waste in the nearest ditch. Such abuses were widespread. As a result, the citizen coalitions around NAFTA and WTO began to demand, among other things, that firms operating under the rules of trade agreements like NAFTA and WTO should be subject to some standards of both labor rights and environmental regulations. Governments, including the U.S. Government, and industry groups like The Chamber of Commerce and the U.S. Business Roundtable, fiercely resisted these demands.

Our demands for environmental and economic justice were labeled "protectionist." It was charged that environmental and labor standards were simply a guise for keeping firms from leaving the U.S. Such protectionism, the argument went, would lead to "inefficiency" and would prevent workers in Mexico, Vietnam, Korea, China and other places from getting jobs that would raise their standard of living. It soon became clear to me that the demands for labor and environmental standards contradicted the whole point of the trade agreements. These agreements were a vital part of the strategy of the New World

Order. And the point of that strategy was to reduce claims on value by reducing production costs, including wages and the cost of preventing further environmental degradation.

In making our case for the need to impose standards on the newly mobile firms, fellow economists were no help at all. In, fact a group of well-known economists published a full-page ad in the New York Times supporting NAFTA and WTO and denouncing opponents and advocates of labor and environmental standards. That got my attention. These economists were influenced by the branch of economics called "environmental economics," and their approach has influenced the profession as a whole. Economists have been highly supportive of the entire New World Order project. The field of economics generally, including environmental economics, bases much of its analysis on a hierarchy of concerns. At the top of the heap is efficient production. Efficiency, in this context, means the lowest possible cost of each item produced. The next step down the ladder is consumption: how to get people in the economy to buy the stuff that is efficiently produced. The third rung down the ladder is the condition of the people; last and certainly least is nature.

In fact, to most mainstream economists, the function of the three bottom rungs of their ladder of concerns is to serve an economy based on efficient production. A healthy economy is one in which output grows. Growth in total output, measured as gross domestic product (GDP), is considered a key indicator of whether economic policy is working properly. Analytically, most economists consider the economy to be an "open system" operating outside of nature. Such an analysis begins with the notion of a circular flow of economic activity. Businesses produce stuff and pay workers wages and salaries. These incomes flow to households and other businesses that buy stuff from the businesses, passing the income back. The vicious circle continues indefinitely, getting larger and larger (economic growth). Theoretically there are no limits to how much an economy can grow. The only things that can limit growth, in this view, are excessive regulation, taxes paid to government and not enough income for people to buy the stuff produced. Government policy is directed at these stumbling blocks. Environmental regulation is secondary to economic growth.

While debating those who supported the trade agreements, it often struck me that scattering production around the world accomplishes two things. First, production becomes more "efficient" by lowering the costs of labor and environmental regulation. Secondly, by making factory workers out of those subsisting on family farms in countries such as Mexico, India and China, the system as a whole can increase consumption levels. The U.S. has the highest levels of per capita consumption in the world. A goal of the New World Order strategy to save capitalism is to bring other nations' levels of per capita consumption up to that of the U.S. And many economists seem to feel that this would be just fine. Environmental economists believe in encouraging growth with minimum regulations using environmental friendly technologies. But, I discovered, there is an alternative view.

A number of economists, biologists, physicists and other scientists concerned with environmental degradation have developed a very different way of examining the relationship of the environment to the economy. They call it ecological economics. (See the work of Herman Daly, one of the founders of ecological economics.) These economists begin their analysis by observing that the economy is surrounded and contained by the

52

ecosystem in which we use solar-based energy to create things we need to live on—food, housing, clothes, etc. The process of living and consuming creates pollution and waste that can be absorbed by the ecosystem and rendered harmless. Oxygen in lakes and rivers, for example, can break down many organic pollutants. Garbage can be composted and turned into soil. *But there is a limit to how much the ecosystem can absorb in a given period of time.* Ecological economists make it clear this limit is the earth's "*carrying capacity.*" If pollution and waste are discharged at a rate that exceeds the earth's *carrying capacity*, environmental degradation in the form of polluted air and water, acid rain, global warming etc. can occur. Herman Daly has cited three factors that can lessen (or accelerate) such degradation. They are population, consumption per person, and technologies that can reduce the degrading impacts of the growth of population and per capita consumption.

Ecological economists make it clear that there are limits to economic growth. This puts them at odds with those who practice environmental economics. The latter seek to lessen negative environmental consequences using both technologies like solar and wind power, smoke stack scrubbers and institutionalized market incentives such as carbon emission trading. The mainstream approach of environmental economics seeks to enable the economy to grow without inhibiting population growth, per capita consumption, and without regulations that cannot be justified by a cost benefit analysis that assumes efficient production.

I find the approach of *ecological economics* persuasive. The idea that there are ecological limits on economic growth seems to be born out by the science we have at our disposal. Most scientists agree, for example, that putting carbon dioxide into the air more quickly than the sun can clean it up has negative consequences for our climate. Certain mining processes deplete resources faster than they can be naturally replaced, and they generate pollutants that poison streams and water tables. Industrial fishing can deplete fishing stocks faster than natural growth can occur. Large-scale farming can and has depleted soil productivity and led to soil erosion. Putting sulfur dioxide and nitrogen oxides into the air by burning coal and running gas-guzzling cars and trucks has created acid rain that is harmful to forests, many plants and fish. But capitalism requires every firm to produce on an expanded basis and at the lowest possible cost. Economic growth requires expanded consumption for each person in society. So there is a contradiction between the health of the environment and the capitalist system.

Historically the worst impacts of that contradiction have been improved or lessened by various government regulations. But the New World Order strategy to save capitalism has heightened the contradiction. Changes in manufacturing technology, transportation technology, mobile financial capital, and the creation of a "free trade" regime combined to break up the manufacturing process and scatter it around the world. Because production was no longer concentrated in industrial nations like the U.S., the task of regulation became international.

The industrial and financial elites and their governments successfully resisted efforts to place any meaningful environmental restrictions on the movement of industrial development. In fact, a number of trade agreements contained clauses that gave firms the right to sue nations that enacted regulations that raised production costs. As a result, there have been a number of successful suits against nations with environmental regulations that reduced company profits. These have been litigated in international tribunals that are outside of the reach of any nation state.

Moreover, it used to be possible to justify environmental regulations using the *precautionary principle* (if you suspect some practice or level of toxic emissions might be harmful, don't do it). That idea is now considered outmoded and its use can result in a lawsuit under international trade regulations. Instead, a justification has to be proved using techniques that demonstrate that the benefit of regulation in dollar terms is greater than the economic costs it imposes.

The New World Order logic has run head-on into the warnings of environmentalists and the adherents to ecological economic research. The result has been political wrangling in a number of nations over whether global warming is natural or man made, whether we can prove the droughts, storms and melting polar ice caps are due to specific environmental practices or are natural. There is a push to squeeze more oil out of sand and shale, engage in environmentally risky drilling, and use so-called "clean coal," etc. Meanwhile, per capita consumption in nations like China, India, Korea, Vietnam, Mexico and Brazil are rising and industrial nations continue to resist significant limits on carbon emissions. Global warming, polluted water and air and bulging land fills are evidence that the limits of economic growth in this New World Order have been surpassed.

Discussion Questions

1. What are key features of the New World Order and how does this system differ from the system that prevailed between 1946 and 1980?
2. Why does the author argue that the development of a New World Order was *not* a conspiracy hatched by a handful of powerful people? Do you agree with his assessment?
3. What are some of the technological developments that made the New World Order possible?
4. What were some of the political/institutional changes that opened up the New World Order?
5. In what sense has debt become both fictitious capital and a fictitious product?
6. What relationship does the author see between the New World Order and the degradation of the environment? Do you agree?

Chapter 4
The Self Destruction of the
New World Order

"It's all a fantasy. A figment. A façade. A phantasm. A false
front. A fata morgana. And frankly it frightens me."

David Ives, *Enigma Variations*

We are presently in a state of "churning and flailing" that is
due to the onset of the historical *crisis of value*. The crisis is itself
the culmination of a contradiction inherent in capitalism. But its
concrete form reflects the specific characteristics of the radical
restructuring that occurred in the 1970s and early 1980s that I have
previously described. The actions of politicians and our society's
elites constitute an effort to hang onto the privileges the New
World Order has bestowed on them. Yet because we are
experiencing the appearance of a contradiction, their interventions
in markets and government policies are causing the crisis to
deepen further. In this sense the day-to-day activities of our
society's elites and the institutions they have created are
contributing to the self-destruction of the New World Order.

1. Markets and the Self Destruction of the Capitalist World Order

Political and business elites are telling us that markets provide the most efficient solutions to the pressing problems of unemployment, poverty, homelessness, declining educational achievement, lack of adequate health care. Indeed, efficiently functioning markets are essential to the survival of capitalism. However, global capitalism today has reached a point where the very features that in theory make markets efficient are disappearing. Markets, to be efficient, must be competitive. Yet, competition has been greatly compromised under the terms of the New World Order. *Such markets increase claims on value without contributing to the production of that value.*

Finally, the trade of these fictitious or phantom goods replaces markets for many of the essentials of everyday life, like housing, food, and automobile gasoline. The price of housing, food and gasoline is not determined primarily by the supply and demand for these items, but by the trade of fictitious commodities—so-called derivatives—that purport to represent their value. The need we all have for life's essentials is thus trumped by the desire of wealthy people to accumulate a fantastic or fictional representation of these things.

Below I will first offer a very brief summary of the theory behind the notion that competitive markets for vital goods and services are central to the functioning of the capitalist system. Then I will turn to how markets have been functioning since the early 1980's and explain how these markets contribute to the self-destruction of the New World Order.

a. **Markets in Theory**

Earlier I argued that the point of capitalism is to accumulate a surplus of values that can be used to reproduce the system and make it grow. In order to do this, owners of private businesses need to have people working for them who produce more value than is required for their own reproduction. Each individual capitalist is driven by competition to attempt to gain the highest rate of profit at the lowest possible cost. The mechanism behind competition is the structure of the specific markets through which useful goods and services are bought and sold.

There have been markets since human beings gathered in settlements to produce goods that could be traded to people producing other goods. Over three thousand years ago, Phoenicians who came from what is now Lebanon developed trade routes along the Mediterranean Sea and up the Western coast of Spain. They established trading posts—physical markets—along the way. More than a thousand years before Christianity and Islam, they founded the city now called Cadiz, Spain, as one of these trading posts. North Africans, Greeks and the Romans, whose empires created markets throughout what we now consider Europe, North Africa and the Middle East, came after the Phoenicians. There were similar developments in Asia.

These markets had very different characteristics, but they were all the creation of "government." It was the state that dictated the structure and the rules under which markets operated, and it was the state that protected them with vast armies and navies. Initially, goods were exchanged through a system of barter. Luxury goods such as gold, jewelry, and later, coins, facilitated trade by representing the exchange value of all the goods in the market. From this development, money became the universal equivalent of all the goods traded in these markets.

Money, in both ancient and modern markets, has no value outside of the relative values of goods and services being exchanged in those markets. And prices are the money form of these values. When there is universal agreement that money is the medium of exchange, it can be used to store value. It becomes a measure of wealth but it still has no intrinsic value apart from what it can be used to buy.

Modern capitalist markets are also created and maintained by governments. The purpose of governmental rules that govern markets is to facilitate the continuation of the capitalist system. When individual capitalists or small groups of capitalists act in such a way that the system as a whole is threatened, the State has historically stepped in with more regulation and more rules. The rules laid down by government provide a structure in which the actions of each individual business owner enable the system as a whole to function in a way that keeps the system going.

Here, in theory, is how it all works: The key mechanism that enables markets to govern the system (within the rules laid out by government) is competition. Each individual business owner attempts to maximize profits. Given this motivation, competition forces each capitalist to invest in technologies and run their businesses in such a way that they maximize the productivity of labor and minimize costs. If they don't do this, a competitor can sell goods or services at a lower price, which will drive the higher cost firm out of business.

What does a "competitive market" mean? First of all, there have to be enough firms and consumers selling and buying in the market so that no single firm, buyer or even small group of them can influence the price. If a small group has the market power to influence price, the incentive for business owners to operate efficiently is undermined. A second characteristic of a competitive market is that the products or services included in the market have to be comparable from the point of view of the person who wishes to buy them. Economists call this criterion a "homogeneous product." A consumer, in making choices between products, has to be able to compare one company's product to another. Thirdly, there can't be any restrictions on new firms or potential consumers from entering markets. Access to markets means there are always potentially new competitors who can increase competition among producers. Also, access for new consumers means a potential for expanding the size and geographical range of markets. And finally, all parties participating in markets have to have enough information about prices of materials, available technology, and the nature of the product or service to be able to make rational choices.

I argue that the markets for some of our most needed goods and services bear little resemblance to these theories. And they are in fact operating in a manner that contributes to the self-destruction of the present system. In many markets a handful of firms dominate sales and thus have the market power to control prices. Historically, there has always been a tendency for a few firms to gain control of particular markets. What makes today's situation unique is the fact that concentration of market power is occurring in the context of the New World Order.

The globalization of manufacturing has given rise to huge retail complexes like Walmart, which can source products from all over the world and dictate wholesale prices to manufacturers. Market power in the retail sector and the ability of large corporations to produce in areas of the world where workers can be paid below the cost of their own subsistence are what determines prices on the supply side. This reality stands in stark contrast to the simplistic economics model of supply and demand, where competition, manufacturers' costs and the demands of "sovereign consumers" drive owners of manufacturing and service firms to the most efficient practices and the lowest possible prices. Further, the need to boost consumer demand while diminishing labor's share of total value production has created an array of phantom markets and phantom "products" that create claims on value but create no value themselves. In many cases they are completely divorced from goods and services required by people for survival and ultimately, reproduction. Only a few major players control these phantom markets, and they have become so complex that even those who create the phantom products and those who buy and sell them have a limited understanding of what they really are.

b. Competition in the Real World

In the U.S. today and in many parts of the world, the structures of markets for many vital goods and services lack a high degree of competitiveness. This does not mean there is no competition. It means that the structure of markets does not ensure that they always operate as efficiently as economic theory and many conservatives proclaim. In the U.S., the government's Economic Census measures the competitiveness of U.S. firms every five years. But they use only one of the criteria listed above—the number of firms that are competing in each market—using a measure called a *concentration ratio*. Economic activities are divided into "industries," like computers, automobiles, and national commercial banks. These industries approximate a market for those products and services. The concentration ratio is the percentage of total sales or shipments in the entire industry accounted for by the largest four firms and the largest eight firms. Looking at these data, competition in many of these industries is quite limited. (All data is taken from the U.S. Bureau of Census Economic Census: www.census.gov/econ/concentration)

In the case of food, the top four breakfast cereal manufacturers account for 78% of all sales. For both poultry processors and commercial bakeries the figure is 46%. The largest four firms account for 43% of the sales of milk. This means that these industries are not particularly competitive. When a few firms can control nearly half of the market or more, they can establish prices with little incentive to produce efficiently. The concentration ratios suggest less than competitive markets for other products and services important to our lives as well. For example, four U.S. firms control 75% of the automobile market. The market for tires has four manufactures accounting for 72% of sales. Four firms account for 80% of the sales of aircraft, which heavily impacts the costs of commercial airlines and ultimately the price of air travel and shipping. In the case of computers, four firms account for 76% of sales.

There is another growing dimension of the concentration of ownership and market power that limits competition. Many household goods in the U.S. and increasingly around the world are purchased from "big box" stores. A few giant retailers like Best Buy dominate electronics. Bed, Bath and Beyond, Crate and

Barrel, IKEA and a few others dominate household items; building materials are sold by giants such as Home Depot and Menards. Drugs and over the counter medicines are dominated by Walgreens, toys by Toys R Us and food by massive supermarket chains. There are also virtual big boxes like Amazon, and thousands of smaller online shopping sites. But the elephant in the big box is Walmart, which increasingly dominates smaller versions of itself like Costco, Sears, K-Mart and Target. In 2005, Walmart had over $285 billion in sales (see Walmart Annual Report). This represented 55% of the sales of the top five big boxes and 22% of the top 20 stores.

The domination of retail sales by the big boxes, and the domination of the big boxes by Walmart have altered the role of retail trade in global capitalism. Walmart is made possible by the fact that they can find products manufactured by cheap labor all over the world. Walmart and some of the others are so big that they have the ability to set prices. Walmart regularly engages in "predatory pricing" which means selling products below production cost to draw in customers and drive out competition. Once the other sellers are out of business, the prices go up.

Walmart's size also means they can afford to sell below their own costs for an extended period of time. Their size and market reach also enables them to dictate prices to the producers, refusing to carry products that don't meet their price demands. This tends to drive some producer firms out of business and forces others to produce their products in the lowest cost regions in the world. Currently, most of Walmart's sales are products produced by labor in China. Thus the retail sector, dominated by Walmart and a few others, are dominating both the supply chains of production and decision-making by the manufactures themselves. And as the big box firms dominate retail sales as well, they dictate market outcomes in a process that is separated from both the costs of production and even the income of consumers. The price of a tube of toothpaste is no longer determined by the costs of its production and a consumer's desire, constrained by income, to purchase it. This contradicts the common sense notion that capitalist markets made the best possible decisions based on efficient competitive production and rational consumers bidding in a market place. Generally, the lack of competition in today's global capitalist markets challenges common sense.

The limited competitiveness of many markets in the U.S. is nothing new. But the tendency today toward a few firms controlling markets for vital goods and services is very different. Markets exist in a global context where the simple textbook notions of supply and demand no longer apply. Nor does the theoretical notion of sovereign consumers and individual producers making intelligent decisions about producing and consuming. Moreover, the particular example of Walmart and the big box stores also represents another specific feature of today's global markets. Increasingly, markets are becoming phantasms by separating themselves from the goods and services that generate value. As production and pricing decisions are driven by retail giant marketing strategies, market fundamentals for the goods and services they sell are pushed aside. But there are other phantom markets that are even more removed from the production of value.

c. **Markets Without Products**

Other types of phantom markets are those that have become removed altogether from the buying and selling of goods and services These are markets without products. Case in point is the practice of a government creating markets and/or market-based incentives to solve social problems. Market approaches to health care reform, public education, and vouchers that privatize public services like public housing are all examples. In a capitalist market-based economy, the government provides goods and services when society determines they should be provided for everyone and markets can't do the job. There are private markets for security services, education, health care and housing. But income constraints mean that without a public sector for these services, a substantial number of citizens are excluded. As a result, in the U.S., we have developed a substantial public sector in these areas. For most people, government provides police, fire protection and education. And for some of the lowest income citizens, there is a social safety net that offers public housing, health care and food.

But as the *crisis of value* becomes greater, the transfer of value to government in the form of taxes increasingly dries up. So politicians and policy wonks attempt to find ways to create fantastic markets that can sidestep the whole problem. Housing vouchers and charter schools offer the appearance of the market mechanism at work. But they paper over the basic problem that government services now constitute a greater claim on the value produced by the system than the system is able to produce. As a result, the social objectives behind public education and housing are lost in the shuffle. And since the ultimate result is that families and individuals can be left out or underserved, the market mechanism becomes the basis for exclusion. For this reason I consider privatization a mechanism for creating markets without products for many citizens.

David Ranney

There are other practices in which the creation of phantom markets to address social problems leaves those problems behind and generates schemes to make money (not value) out of thin air. A prime example is the policy of "cap and trade," used to address the problem of thick carbon-laden air that has been linked to global warming. Markets have been created for the right of companies to pollute the air with global warming-inducing greenhouse gasses. Paradoxically, the idea behind such schemes is to offer "free market" financial incentives to actually reduce pollution globally.

From the 1990's until today, various nations and groups of nations have established limits on the number of tons of carbon dioxide (CO2) or CO2-equivalent gasses that a company or nation may emit in a given time period. Having established these limits known as "caps," tradable certificates are issued to firms and governments that are below the cap, giving them the right to emit the greenhouse gasses up to the limit. Each certificate is usually worth one ton of pollutants. These can be sold either to firms who are above their limits, or to companies, investment funds or exchanges that then trade them on open markets. The certificates, which have no value in and of themselves, are nevertheless bought and sold in markets at prices determined by their supply and demand. If the sales price is sufficiently high, the theory is that it will become profitable for big gas emitters who have bought lower-priced certificates to sell them and invest some of the proceeds in emission-reducing technology. Since there is no real product or service being bought or sold, notions about the efficiency of free markets go up in carbon-laden smoke, and all sorts of side effects can occur.

For example, it was recently discovered that nineteen firms in India and China that produce a highly toxic, carbon related gas, began to produce an excess of the gas and then destroy it. They were compensated for their efforts in the form of carbon credit certificates and then sold them on the open market, making a handsome profit. For some firms this has grown to more than half of their total profits, bringing in between $20-40 million a year. So, a more than $60 billion phantom market without a real product has been created. Money without value is created out of polluted air. (*Incentive to Slow Climate Change Drives Output of Harmful Gases*, New York Times, August 9, 2012.)

Another example of a phantom market has emerged out of the U.S. life insurance industry. Many people take some of the value they have created and invest it in life insurance. Today the total value of all active life insurance policies is $18 trillion. This amount comes out of the current income of the policyholders. The $18 trillion is thus a claim on the value generated by the capitalist system. The amount policyholders pay for premiums each year is based on their life expectancy and the size of their death benefits. The calculation of premiums is designed so the company makes a substantial profit. In addition, insurance companies make money by investing the premiums. They also make a substantial portion of their profits from policyholders who stop making payments by canceling the policy before they die. The company gets all of the payments made but does not have to pay death benefits. Many people cancel their policies due to lack of income or because the beneficiary of the policy has died.

The windfall from cancelled policies is a sizable amount of money, and new phantom markets have been formed to exploit it. Participants call it "life settlements" which is a gentle way of saying it is a market for early death. It all started with the AIDS epidemic. In the early days of the appearance of the disease there was no treatment available. Contracting AIDS meant death in a few years, at most. Large numbers of people who had contracted AIDS—mostly gay men at that time—found themselves with this horrible disease and no funds for their own care, or even living expenses, at the end of their life.

Someone came up with the idea of buying their life insurance policies. A "life settlement" buyer would offer cash to people with AIDS for their insurance policies, along with a contract requiring the buyer to continue paying premiums until the seller's death. The buyer would then become the beneficiary of the death benefits from the policy he or she bought. The longer the seller of the policy lived, however, the less money the buyer would make because of the cost of premium payments. So in a sense the buyer was hoping for the shortest possible life for the seller of the policy. When new drugs for AIDS began to prolong life potential profits for consumers in the life settlement market were substantially lowered. So a new wrinkle was added to the structure of this phantom market.

Brokerage firms were set up to buy and sell the policies of large numbers of old or sick policyholders who needed immediate cash. They would then sell a group of policies to individual investors or investment funds that would spread the risk of people living too long! This has become a substantial phantom market. It has been estimated that 40% of all seniors in the U.S. have either surrendered their policies or let payments lapse. In 2007 the total value of these life settlements was $12 billion. That number is projected to grow to $148 billion by 2019. By contrast, in 2010, actual death benefits paid amounted to only 3.8 billion.

(James Vlahos, *Are You Worth More Dead Than Alive?* New York Times Magazine, August 12, 2012, pp. 30-35.)

Phantom markets for things like carbon credits and life settlements, where there are no products or vital services, are growing and creating the illusion of wealth. It is an illusion because the appearance of wealth has no relation to value, and value is needed to keep the capitalist system going. While some individuals get rich, their wealth is not sustainable. Because these markets draw on value created elsewhere and put nothing back into the economy, they are a pure claim on value. And since the *crisis of value* we are experiencing is a crisis caused by greater claims on value production than the system can generate, profits from carbon credits and life settlements are actually contributing to the system's self destruction. But the growth of uncompetitive markets, as well as phantom markets without products, are only a small part of the contribution of today's market structures to the deepening of the *crisis of value*. The jumbo elephants in the room are the derivative markets.

d. Phantom Derivative Markets

Earlier, I described the evolution of a New World Order as a major reorganization of global capitalism that occurred in the 1970s and 1980s. I emphasized that its goal was to reduce labor's share of value production as a way out of the *crisis of value* at that time. But this gave rise to another contradiction. As labor's share of value declined, the ability of working class people to purchase goods and services needed for their survival and reproduction declined. Yet the New World Order form of the capitalist system depended on the working class continuing to buy goods and services in order to realize value, and reproduce themselves as well as the system.

The solution—very temporary as it turned out—was to encourage debt. Led by credit cards and student loans, household debt skyrocketed. Even with less income, workers could still buy stuff. They could also buy houses they couldn't afford using subprime mortgages. And because governments are financed by taxes that come from labor's share of value, government revenues declined and government debt spiked as well. The inducement for lenders to make loans under such shaky circumstances was to make debt a commodity in its own right. Earlier I referred to such debt as both fictitious capital and a fictitious product. A market for debt was created through an existing market known as *derivatives*.

Derivatives may be defined as pieces of paper or even computer entries whose prices are roughly based on the price of something else. Derivatives markets began innocently enough and on a very modest scale. The initial form of derivatives was the "futures contract." The Chicago Board of Trade, where much of this sort of trading originated, was established as a grain exchange in 1848. The idea was to bring together speculators who would buy grain contracts that would specify prices at some future date. Farmers and others who needed certainty about future prices could sell these contracts to speculators who were betting they could ultimately resell them at a higher price. This was always a phantom market because the consumers of this "product" by and large had no need or desire for grain or any other commodity. They were essentially making a profit by buying and selling contracts above the value of the commodity.

Gradually, a variety of other commodities were added to the derivative markets. And eventually traders began trading futures in financial assets. This development was an essential feature of the New World Order because it could transform growing debt into a commodity. Lenders were induced to lend because they knew they could turn around and sell the debt. Initially the focus was on government debt. The future prices of government bonds, and municipal bonds and notes (short term government debt) are examples. But this principle extended to foreign debt as well. In the early 1970s, financial futures were less than 1% of the Chicago Board of Trade (CBOT) business. By 1980 this had risen to 20%; by 2000 the figure was over 80%. Debt trading had become a significant business. (*CBOT sources.*)

Initially, this trading was largely done on exchanges like the Chicago Board of Trade, The Chicago Mercantile Exchange, the Chicago Board of Options Exchange and their counterparts in other cities around the world. In the U.S., the exchanges were carefully monitored and regulated. But as the financial derivatives markets grew, investment banks, which were limited to playing with rich people's money, got into the act. The investment bank trading of financial derivatives was known as "over the counter trading."

As I discussed earlier, the government regulations that prevented investment banks from dipping into business and citizen depositors' money was eliminated in 1999, the year the Gramm-Leach-Bliley Act replaced the Depression era Glass Steagall Act. This immediately resulted in the legalization of a mega-merger of investment, insurance and commercial banking giants: Citicorp, Travelers Insurance, Salomon-Smith Barney. A new firm called Citigroup was born. This deregulation and subsequent merger generated other similar mergers throughout the U.S. Giant financial entities began trading private debt in what became an enormous business of over the counter trading (OTC) of private debt. And OTC trading was practically immune to government oversight. As this business exploded, major banks around the world began to join financial derivatives trading markets. Another key piece of deregulation—the Commodity Futures Modernization Act of 2000—opened things even further by specifically exempting over the counter trades from regulation.

Mergers and further deregulation encouraged "too big to fail" finance houses to come up with even more creative "products." Debt of varying qualities and type were merged into "collateralized debt obligations" or CDOs. Insurance firms like AIG began selling insurance policies against the default of the CDOs (called credit default swaps) on the false assumption that the entire content of a CDO could not default at the same time. Then even the credit default swaps became products that were traded in these markets.

If the price of derivatives is supposedly derived from some underlying asset like the value of a bushel of corn, a house, a car or higher education, the CDOs were actually derivatives of other derivatives. In the aftermath of the collapse of these markets, it was revealed that most of the buyers and sellers had no clear idea of what was in them. A credit default swap as an insurance policy against a CDO default is even more removed from the contents of the CDO. And a credit default swap that is traded as a product in its own right is pure phantasm.

In the film *Margin Call*, based on the collapse of Lehman Brothers, the CEO (played by Jeremy Irons) has decided to dump

CDOs on the market to minimize losses after a young analyst discovers that the mortgages inside the CDOs are defaulting. He concluded that the CDOs would soon be worthless. His closest associate objects to dumping the CDOs because they would be knowingly selling things that are worthless. Iron's character responds: "You've been around here long enough to realize that none of this is real. All we do is buy and sell pieces of paper with designs and pictures on them. They are worth whatever people think they're worth." That about sums it up. But real or not the market for financial derivatives is huge, while being both opaque and highly concentrated in a few greedy hands.

In terms of size, one has to be careful when looking at the numbers reported on various websites. This is because they use different measures and don't always specify their sources. A good source is the Bank of International Settlements (BIS), which collects data quarterly from member banks. Banks from 43 nations submit reports to BIS. At the end of 2011, the price value of the assets represented by all of the derivatives contracts in the world (called notional value by the finance people) was about $800 trillion. (*BIS Quarterly Report*, June 2012.) About 10% of this amount was purchased in regulated commodity exchanges like the Chicago Board of Trade. The other 90% were so-called over the counter trades (OTC), which were traded by unregulated investment banks. One report on these markets estimates the size to be even higher, at $1,200 trillion or $1.2 quadrillion (Peter Cohan, *Big Risk: $1.2 Quadrillion Derivatives Market Dwarfs World GDP* www.dailyfinance.com/2010/06/09/) With numbers this big it hardly matters. You might as well say a gazillion!

The size of all these markets, whatever measure we use, is far greater than the entire gross domestic product (a measure of the size of national economies) of the whole world. The world GDP now stands at around $65 trillion. (www.data.worldbank.org) If the derivatives market is around $800 trillion, it amounts to more than twelve times the size of the output of the entire world in a single year.

Adding to this fantastic stew is the fact that banks use their derivative positions as collateral to purchase other derivatives, other assets, or to take huge positions in other markets without any money at all. When the big banks went down it was revealed that many giant financial institutions had leveraged the purchase of their investments up to 20-1. This means they could buy $20 dollars worth of phantom products for only $1! The risk of this practice was covered by yet another derivative. They bought insurance policies, called credit default swaps (at a leverage rate of between 15 and 20-1), from insurance giants like American Insurance Group (AIG) against the default of the debt represented by the derivative. This only expanded the size of the derivatives market and the growing risk involved when something of no value purports to represent the value of an underlying asset, like housing.

Furthermore, financial derivatives markets are not in the least competitive. In the U.S., four banks account for about 96% of the U.S. share of this market (Tyler Durden, *Five Banks Account For 96% of the $250 Trillion In Outstanding U.S. Derivative Exposure,* 9/2/2011 www.zerohedge.com. Durden's numbers come from the U.S. Office of the Currency Comptroller.) There are no "homogenous products" involved. It is impossible to compare various "products" and make informed choices because the markets are completely opaque. When giants like Lehman Brothers went down it was clear that its top executives, including the risk management people, hadn't a clue about what was in their hedge funds, where many of the derivatives were located. (A good account of this is reported in *The Big Short*, by Michael Lewis.)

The products that made up these markets were always phantom products operating in phantom markets—the buyers and sellers had no interest in the products underlying the derivatives. They were never in a market that was subject to the Economics 101 version of supply and demand. But with the emergence of CDOs and credit default swaps the separation of these markets from reality became total. And the fiction they represented became a fiction on an unprecedented grand and global scale.

But most importantly the buying and selling of phantasms was needed to implement the New World Order strategy to save capitalism in the wake of the *crisis of value* of the 1970s. Deregulation opened the door for these trades. And the resulting "too big to fail" financial institutions created the phantom markets and products that enabled the New World Order to function. The New World Order strategy deliberately diminished labor's share of the production of global value. But because the reorganized capitalist system still needed labor's buying power, lending was expanded to those with low wages who would not previously have been credit worthy. There was also a need to expand credit to governments whose reduced revenues were a by-product of the destruction of labor's share of value production. Derivative markets that turned debt into a commodity that could be bought and sold made this extension of credit possible. Derivative markets for debt were, and still are, essential to the system's survival. But because they create claims on value without creating any value, they feed the *crisis of value* we presently face. For this reason, they are a part of the self-destruction of today's New World Order.

This contradiction is embedded in the derivatives markets themselves, and it is heightened as these markets, despite operating independently of the goods and services they are linked to, influence prices in a number of the underlying markets. In doing so they have ultimately contributed to homelessness, hunger and even starvation. So I now turn to the impact of some derivatives markets on the prices of housing and food.

e. Phantom Derivatives Markets: the Case of Housing

The government created a program to start the first derivatives markets for housing mortgages two crises ago, during the Great Depression. At that time most home mortgages came from Savings and Loan Associations (S&Ls). People put their savings in the bank and the S&L lent some of those savings to people who needed credit to buy a home or to purchase cars or major appliances. To get a mortgage on a house, it was necessary to come up with a down payment of 20-30% of the market price of the home. The borrower also had to demonstrate an ability to make the payments. Home mortgages were an important part of the S&L business. A healthy housing industry was also a key to any hope for recovery from the Great Depression, as the Bretton Woods-post World War II reorganization of the global capitalist system got underway.

In order to protect those who made deposits into S&Ls and other banks, the government required that banks keep a certain percentage of their deposits in the bank. So financial institutions that depended on bank deposits to offer mortgages and other loans had only a limited amount to lend. In some parts of the U.S., especially rural areas and other places where the volume of savings was limited, there was not enough credit available for people who could otherwise afford to buy houses. With the demand for mortgages high relative to the supply of funds, the government stepped in and helped facilitate the development of what are known as secondary mortgage markets. A process was established through which lenders could sell their outstanding mortgages to investors, providing a source of money that could be lent to other mortgage seekers. This greatly expanded the amount of credit available for the purchase of homes. At the same time it integrated real estate with a growing number of other financial "products" that constituted capital markets at that time.

Here's how it worked. After World War II, special institutions were created, initially government institutions, known as "conduits." Conduits were meant to facilitate the movement of mortgages from the lender to the portfolios of investors, such as pension funds and mutual funds. The conduit did this by pooling a group of mortgages with similar characteristics (interest rates, the time period of the loan, type of property, financial capacity of the borrower) and using this pool to back a security or bond that could be bought and sold in securities markets similar to the way stocks and bonds are traded. The bonds gave bondholders the right to draw on a portion of the principle and interest payments on the mortgages in the pool. The legal documents for each individual home mortgage in the bond pool were placed in a trust until the mortgages were paid off to the investors holding the securities. These mortgage-backed securities (MBSs) could be bought and sold like any stock or bond.

The original government conduit was the Federal National Mortgage Association known as "Fannie Mae." Established in 1935 as part of the New Deal, its secondary market activity was initially limited to remote rural areas that were strapped for funds to make mortgage loans. Fannie Mae's original conduit activity was also limited to mortgages that carried government guarantees from the Federal Housing Administration (FHA) and the Veterans Administration (VA).

As a new *crisis of value* began to appear in the late sixties, legislation was enacted to expand the secondary mortgage markets. In 1968, a new law included provisions that constituted a major breakthrough, integrating FHA and VA guaranteed mortgages with the broader housing markets. Fannie Mae was privatized into a public corporation that could issue stock. Many big players in the financial markets participated.

The 1968 act also created a second corporation, the General National Mortgage Association, known as Ginnie Mae. Ginnie Mae's function was to guarantee the mortgages in Fannie Mae's pool. Despite that fact that the FHA and VA already guaranteed these mortgages, a general default of a mortgage-backed security could mean holders of the securities had long delays before getting their investment back. Because the FHA and VA guaranteed each individual mortgage in the bonds, they had to review each mortgage to determine the extent of their liability. This took time. Ginnie Mae guaranteed the entire pool and absorbed the cost of any potential time delay, making mortgage-based securities even more marketable in the financial markets.

In 1970, the federal government created a third secondary market institution. The Federal Home Loan Mortgage Corporation

(Freddie Mac) was established to create pools of conventional mortgages (those not guaranteed by the government), which at that time constituted nearly 80% of all mortgages. This development expanded secondary market activity even further.

The creation of a secondary mortgage market through the establishment of Fannie Mae, Ginnie Mae and Freddie Mac, although created prior to the evolution of the New World Order, provided a necessary precondition for turning the secondary mortgage market into a huge global phantasm. By the mid 1990s, Fannie Mae and Freddie Mac held over $1 trillion in outstanding mortgages. In 1995, Fannie Mae made a profit of $2.1 billion on its secondary market operations. The profit potential coupled with the risk aversion mechanisms provided by Ginnie Mae seemed an unlimited opportunity to the financial world. This brought the hedge funds, pension funds and even governments into the game on a huge scale. The largest investment banks—many which merged with commercial banks after deregulation—operated these hedge funds. They also created, bought and speculated directly on mortgage-backed securities. Goldman Sachs and Citigroup, along with Merrill Lynch, Lehman Brothers, Bear Stearns, Wells Fargo, Morgan Stanley, Bank of America, Deutschebank, UBS, and many others around the world entered the arena of the secondary mortgage and debt markets.

The resulting explosion of a market of such size and potential led to a number of private sector "innovations" that began to drive not only the secondary mortgage markets, but housing markets as well. The massive secondary mortgage market and other debt markets resulted in practically unlimited credit. The demand for mortgage-backed securities caused lenders to expand the number of primary mortgage recipients. As a result, credit began to drive the demand for housing—especially at the lower (less expensive) end of the housing market. With greater demand, the price of housing increased and this stimulated the supply of housing. Ultimately, housing prices were not driven by the labor that went into the houses (their value) nor even by housing supply and demand. *Rather, increasing prices for housing reflected the supply and demand for the mortgage-backed securities in the secondary market.* (One of the best explanations of the "innovations" in the secondary market and what happened in these markets up to their collapse in 2009 is Michael Lewis' book *The Big Short*. I am basing part of my explanation on his work.)

Explaining the many innovations in housing derivatives is beyond the scope of this book. But I do want to highlight a number of them in order to make the point that prior to the 2008-9 collapse, housing markets had become a pure phantasm. The innovations came in response to institutional roadblocks regarding the size, speed, and risk to profit flows in the housing derivatives markets. As investors and speculators poured into these markets, the number of individual mortgages in the pool of mortgages represented by the bonds could be in the thousands.

As mentioned earlier, such a bond gave the bondholder a claim on the cash flows generated by all the mortgages in the pool. Each bond consisted of mortgages of similar quality. They were rated, in terms of risk, by credit rating agencies like Standard and Poor, and Moody's. The lower the quality of mortgages in the pool, the lower the rating. But higher risk pools paid higher interest, and the risk of default on the bond was generally low since the government guaranteed all the mortgages in the pool, and Ginnie Mae paid promptly if an entire bond defaulted.

At this point, investors considered the main risk to be the possibility of homeowners refinancing their homes when interest rates were low. This meant the bondholders got an influx of cash at an inopportune time, reducing cash flow returns on their investment. The solution was to carve up the bond into groups of mortgages (called *traunches*) that were rated according to possible prepayment date. The lowest traunch consisted of mortgages with the earliest prepayment date—they paid the highest interest rate in the entire pool. The next traunch had a lower prepayment risk and paid the bondholder less interest, etc. So prepayment risk was reduced up front by the amount of interest paid.

Eventually the mortgage pool became more mixed, consisting of higher quality guaranteed mortgages and some lower quality mortgages that were not guaranteed. Then the lower traunches that carried the highest risk and highest interest rates included not only high prepayment risk, but also default risk. If the lowest traunch defaulted, the investor simply continued to collect in the next highest traunch. Loss due to default or prepayment had already been compensated for by higher interest collected prior to default or prepayment.

Now that there was a market for low quality mortgages, it stimulated lenders to offer them to people likely to default. As soon as they lent the money, lenders could then sell the mortgages to banks and conduits and get a big return. Hence a subprime mortgage market was created. It was now possible for potential homebuyers with very bad credit ratings and no money to obtain a mortgage without making a down payment.

In the new subprime markets, there were usually two mortgages involved. There was a mortgage that essentially covered the down payment with very low, fixed "teaser" interest rates. Then after about five years, the first mortgage had to be paid off with a second mortgage that had higher, flexible, interest rates. At this point monthly payments could skyrocket. Lewis provided some figures on the size and growth of the sub-prime market. In the mid 1990s, subprime lending was about $30 billion. By 2000, it had grown to $130 billion, half of which was packaged as mortgage-backed securities that paid investors very high rates of interest. By 2005, the amount of subprime lending had grown to $625 billion with $507 billion packaged into bonds. Also, in 2005, 75% of the mortgages in the bonds had floating rates, up from 35% a decade earlier.

An increasing number of mortgages were simply junk. But junk dealing was highly profitable. It is important to realize that almost all of the buying and selling of debt, including the junk, was highly leveraged. That means that purchasers of mortgage-based securities borrowed the money to make the buys. In some cases the leverage was as high as 20-1. They used only $1 of their own money or assets for every $20 worth of stuff they bought.

Junk bonds were not only profitable, they were easy to buy. And the financial houses selling junk made adjustments to make them even more profitable and more marketable. One problem they faced was that the credit ratings of the bonds impacted their marketability. Another was how to manage the risk of default, which was growing. This resulted in two innovations. One was the packaging of mortgage-based securities into another bond called a collateralized debt obligation (CDO).

The CDO had been around for a while. Initially it was used primarily to package large numbers of corporate and government bonds that were not very marketable into a new bond that would sell. A CDO could consist of a hundred or more bonds, each of which consisted of thousands of individual loans. The selling point was the assumption that everything in the CDO wouldn't go bad at the same time. But the use of CDOs expanded to include all sorts of mortgages and other consumer loans. Lewis described the CDO as a "tower." Its lower floors had higher interest rates but a greater probability of default, similar to the mortgage-based securities and their traunches. But the CDO, made up of mortgage-based securities and other loans, eventually became so opaque it was difficult, if not impossible, to see what was inside. Financial houses began to mix higher quality mortgage-based securities with subprime, to the point that sub-prime mortgages were able to get top credit ratings. In some cases, these complex financial packages went from 2% subprimes to 95%.

As discussed earlier, insurance policies on financial investments called "credit default swaps" were also used to manage risk. Initially, these were used for corporate bonds. If you bought a credit default swap that lasted ten years for $100,000 a year, the most it could cost you was a million dollars. But if the bond insured by the credit default swap was worth five million, you would get the cash flows on the bonds plus $5 million if they defaulted. Firms like Goldman Sachs expanded the use of this device. Credit default swaps on crappy mortgage bonds with low credit ratings were packaged and called "synthetic CDOs." The synthetic CDO looked so good that Moody's gave it their highest rating: AAA. In this way, BBB bonds were turned into AAA. In *The Big Short*, a few individuals who saw the folly of this began buying credit default swaps, essentially betting against the insured bonds. Eventually Goldman and others began buying credit default swaps too, betting against products they continued to sell. When the house of cards collapsed, the holders of credit default swaps made a great deal of money. Some, especially AIG Insurance, were left holding a bag of junk.

All this phantom market hocus-pocus had a decided impact in the real world. As easy credit became available to everyone, the government, facing a very real fiscal crisis, began cutting back on housing programs for the poor. The public housing program was eliminated (through privatization), as well as the program that provided subsidies to rental housing developers. Also, lending institutions began pushing sub-prime mortgages. Middle-income people found that instead of paying $150,000 for a home, they could now "afford" one for $250,000. This increased the demand for housing across the board and caused an unprecedented rise in housing prices that most mistook for an increase in value.

There are lots of sources of data on historical housing prices. One of the best is the Case-Shiller housing index. I also consulted data collected by the Center for Economic Policy Research (www.CEPR.net) and J. Parson's housing bubble website (www.jparsons.net/housingbubble/). The data show that in the decade between 1996 and 2006 real (inflation adjusted) median (average) housing prices grew by over 80%. The collapse in housing prices touched off a major recession that exacerbated the collapse of the housing market. Some banks collapsed as well; others were bailed out by our tax dollars. Most importantly, millions of households lost their homes due to foreclosure. As I write this, the Mortgage Banker's Association estimates that every three months 250,000 families enter into foreclosure proceedings.

The housing market mess is a part of the much larger mess of the New World Order system of substituting debt for the creation of value during a *crisis of value*. Making housing debt into a commodity enabled the derivative markets for mortgage debt to dominate the market for housing itself. A series of phantom products in phantom markets evolved from the old mortgage-backed security bond to the synthetic CDO. Thus housing, a product that is vital to our lives, has become beholden to the fictions dreamed up in finance house boardrooms.

f. Phantom Derivatives Markets: The Case of Food

Food is another basic human need that has been invaded by phantom derivatives markets. Its impact is worldwide and plays a role in hunger, famine and starvation. A unique characteristic of food production is that its availability is directly affected by unpredictable weather patterns. It seems to be a simple economic proposition that if the supply of food goes down because of uncontrollable weather events, and the demand stays the same, or even grows with the population its price will go up.

Not so fast! There's more to it than that. The great Nobel economist, Amartya Sen, has taught us that famine and hunger are not simply caused by lack of food. Rather, he argues, social inequalities that determine the way food is distributed have caused famines, hunger and starvation for millions of people. In short, throughout history the human need for food has often been compromised by politics and power.

It's no different today. Massive corporate farms, agribusiness firms that process and distribute food, supermarkets and big box corporations such as Walmart, as well as selective government farm subsidies that protect politically connected businesses, play a very powerful role in global food markets. Hunger in China, the rash of suicides by Indian small farmers and the growing problem of food insecurity are related to these global market forces And they are aided and abetted by the rules of the New World Order institution, The World Trade Organization (WTO).

Hunger in the U.S. is widespread. A recent report issued by the U.S. Department of Agriculture has indicated that 17.2 million households in the U.S. are "food insecure," meaning they lack "consistent, dependable access to enough food for active, healthy living." (Alisha Coleman-Jensen et. al, *Household Food Security in the United States in 2010*, Economic Research Service, U.S. Department of Agriculture, www.ers.usda.gov) 6.4 million households had "very low food security," in which some members of the household were forced to disrupt and/or reduce eating because of a lack of resources to purchase food. 3.9% of households with children experienced very low food security. Very low food security means that some members of the household were going hungry. In U.S. studies, hunger is related to poverty. And poverty, in turn, is related to the fact that many working class families lost considerable income to New World Order policies that eliminated living wage manufacturing jobs. But in addition, increased food insecurity is related to spikes in food prices, and hence to the broader market forces that impact hunger around the world.

During the last decade, world food prices have been quite unstable. Between 2003 and 2008, prices doubled. Corn prices tripled between 2005 and 2008, wheat went up 127% and rice prices increased by 170%. Food prices in general dropped significantly between 2008 and 2009 then rose sharply between 2009 and 2011. (Olivier De Schutter, *Food Commodities Speculation and Food Price Crises,* U.N. Special Rapporteur on the Right to Food included in the Institute for Agriculture and Trade Policy collection *Excessive Speculation in Agriculture Commodities.* www.iatp.org. The data are collected by The United Nations Commission on Trade and Development (UNCTAD) and reported in an annual publication: *UNCTAD Trade and Development Report* as well as regular statistical publications listed on their website as UNCTADSTAT).

The World Bank estimates that the spikes in food prices drove 40 million people worldwide into hunger and deprivation and that there were 960 million people living in hunger in 2008. Since poverty was increasing during much of this period, both in the U.S. and around the world, hunger and food insecurity grew. Contrary to reports from the Organization of Economic Cooperation and Development and the International Monetary Fund, there is sound data that show that the price increases were *not* caused primarily by supply changes due to weather or demand increases from growing middle class populations of India and China. Olivier De Schutter and a number of other authors in the IATP collection cited earlier present evidence that simple supply and demand cannot explain the jump in food prices during the 2003-8 period.

De Schutter and others argue quite convincingly that excessive speculation in food has played a major role. In April 2010, Harper's Magazine published an article by contributing editor Frederick Kaufman, titled *The Food Bubble: How Wall Street starved millions and got away with it.* Kaufman argued that the entry of unregulated "over the counter" financial traders into food derivatives led to over-speculation and unjustifiable spikes in food prices around the world. The weight of evidence presented since that time clearly indicates that the appearance of phantom markets in the food arena had played a very significant role in destabilizing food prices by causing price spikes that have led to hunger. (A good collection of the papers in this debate has been assembled by Steve Suppan of the Institute for Agriculture and Trade Policy: *Excessive Speculation in Agriculture Commodities, Selections from 2008-11*, April, 2011. http://www.iatp.org)

There has been speculation in food markets for a very long time. As I discussed earlier, derivatives originated in the trading of food commodities. But the nature of derivatives trading in food and other commodities has undergone a significant shift since 1991. Prior to that, traditional speculation in food worked like this:

Speculators entered the grain exchanges when they discovered they could make money from the daily fluctuations in real food prices. A speculator who believed that the price of, say, a bushel of corn was apt to go up would buy a futures contract promising to sell corn at some future date at a price higher than existing prices. That contract could be bought and sold by other traders as prices anticipated at the end of the contract period fluctuated in the exchanges. Because none of the speculators had any corn to sell or facilities to store it, they had to match every promise to *buy* future corn (known as a long position) with a promise to *sell* an equal amount (short position).

Many farmers, millers, and big food processors that wanted to reduce the risk of wild price fluctuation by hedging on prices liked this system. They were able to plant corn, or plan for a supply of corn, in a known price range. The steady stream of buy and sell contracts the speculators provided allowed these hedgers to buy and sell real corn as they needed it. They then looked to the futures markets as a guide to the actual price, called the "spot price." Not all corn and other food commodities were traded through futures contracts. But even for corn bought and sold outside of the exchanges, the futures prices became a guide for the whole market. Government regulations kept this process within bounds by limiting the number of futures contracts a speculator could hold at one time. This prevented hoarding. The process tended to stabilize prices, which was good for almost everyone who participated in the system.

However, not everyone had access to these markets. Small farmers and very poor consumers lacked the market power to participate. And they could be hurt if prices fell below the level where small farmers could make a living, or rose above what low-income consumers could afford.

The system worked fairly well, however, for the players on the exchanges. Speculative futures and spot prices of actual food transactions could never get very far apart. When a contract came due, everyone who did not hold equal long and short positions was obligated to buy and sell real corn. This caused futures and spot prices to converge as real food changed hands. In the exchanges, where speculators and hedgers roamed, futures prices historically stayed a little behind spot prices where real food was being bought and sold. This provided a further price guide for those who were actually buying and selling corn and other food commodities. It was also a guide for commodities buyers and sellers outside of the exchanges.

Beginning in 1991 this practice began to decline. The large hedge funds—many belonging to the "too big to fail" financial institutions—felt too constrained by activities in the established futures exchanges. Having to hold both long and short positions and constantly monitor the movement of markets was not to the liking of hedge fund managers who were speculating with mortgages, CDOs, and a variety of other things. They wanted a quicker, more simplified kind of speculation. Also, these hedge fund managers were not used to any government regulation, and the exchange regulations limited potential returns that could spill over into other hedge fund operations. Yet food, being a human need, had too much potential to give up on.

Goldman Sachs and other large financial institutions had been casting hungry eyes on food for some time. In 1991, Goldman came up with a way to speculate on food and other commodities, like oil and minerals, without the constraints of exchange-bound futures contracts. A new "product" was born that they called a "commodity index." The result was so spectacular that Goldman sold the index to none other than Standard and Poors, the very agency that gives financial ratings to bonds, cities and nations. Today the index is known as S&P GSCI. There are similar products owned by Dow Jones, Rogers International Commodities and others. It has become a dominant method through which most commodities are traded.

Instead of buying individual futures for corn, wheat, oil and gold, Goldman traders bought futures of a wide variety of commodities and combined them into what is known as a "commodity fund." Presently, the S&P GSCI includes 23 separate commodities: five types of energy products including crude oil and natural gas, five industrial and two precious metals, eight agricultural commodities (wheat, red wheat, corn, soybeans, cotton, sugar, coffee, cocoa) and three separate livestock commodities. The largest component of the fund is the energy commodities which, taken together, constitute nearly 29% of the fund. Agriculture is only 10.42%. The futures prices of all of these separate commodities are reduced mathematically to a single index number that is based on the weighted futures prices of each commodity. This *number* is then traded outside the exchanges in the over the counter markets where hedge funds, Goldman, and all the other "too big to fail" institutions play.

The traders of the index funds in the exchanges are not trying to make money by buying and selling futures contracts. The real deal is the index number. So they don't match long and short positions. Instead, their portfolios in the exchanges are all "longs," that is, contracts to sell futures. When the contract dates on the futures come due, they sell them and use the proceeds to buy identical sets of futures at an even higher price, purchasing the new futures contracts with hedge fund clients' money. Because the funds include so many different commodities, even regulations limiting the number of futures that a particular commodity a trader can hold were not much of a restriction. Even so, it wasn't long before Goldman and others got to the regulators and gained an exemption from even this regulation for the commodity index funds. Now virtual hoarding was possible and practically unlimited. And since virtual hoarding drove up the spot prices of the actual commodities contained in the index, the result was the same as putting huge amounts of corn in a storage facility to drive up the price.

This changed the entire market for commodity derivatives trading. The mechanisms that kept spot prices slightly above futures prices (called "backwardation" by the famous economist John Maynard Keynes) were gone. As traders continued to push up futures prices, they began to lead spot prices, a tendency that traders call "contango." Constant buying of futures at higher and higher prices caused the real spot prices to rise as well. Meanwhile, the index numbers purchased by hedge fund clients also went up. The returns to the hedge funds were huge. The resulting speculative bubbles in the real commodities markets continued to inflate until the hedge fund traders figured they were ready to burst and allowed them to deflate.

It is through the operations of the commodity index funds and commodity indexes that the same hedge fund managers and financial institutions that manipulated mortgage markets have contributed to world hunger and food riots in many parts of the world. Rising food prices leading to hunger have also played an important role in the "Arab Spring," which brought down governments in Egypt, Tunisia and Libya, and now threatens a number of others. How all of this will play out is not known. But the hedge fund managers continue to fiddle with their index as the world burns.

There is more to this story than housing and food. Crude oil, unleaded gas, heating oil, and natural gas are also included in the commodity indexes. And there is good evidence suggesting that the indexes play an important role in the spikes and general instability in energy prices. A number of policy analysts have made specific proposals for regulation of the trading of these indexes that will fix the problems caused by price instability and distortion. While I certainly favor such proposals, they don't really get at the heart of the problem. And as I write this, the large financial players are generating new phantom markets and phantom products in the commodity markets. A recent report in the *New York Times* revealed that Goldman Sachs, J.P. Morgan Chase and other financial players have been buying up warehouses to store aluminum and copper and are buying oil pipelines. They are moving and storing these commodities in order to make a profit on newly acquired facilities and also to manipulate supply, and hence prices, as they speculate in commodity markets. (David Kocieniewski, *A shuffle of aluminum, but to banks, pure gold*, *New York Times*, July 21, 2013.)

The relentless creation of phantom markets and phantom products happens for a reason beyond simply the greed of financial traders: ***the growth of phantom markets is needed for the present configuration of the global capitalist system to survive.*** Derivative markets for housing and commodities play an important role. At the same time, all the phantom markets I have been discussing contribute to the present *crisis of value* by generating claims on the value being created without contributing to the production of that value. This contradiction is inherent in the capitalist system. But in the churning and flailing that historically accompanies such crises, a variety of forces are attempting to find a way out. Many of these forces are working at cross-purposes. Since my focus is on "The American System," let's turn now to one of these forces—the U.S. Government—to examine its role in the present crisis.

2. Government and the Self Destruction of the New World Order

As the present crisis of value deepens, the churning and flailing that marks every crisis is leaving its mark on politics and government policies in the United States and around the world. Because today's crisis of value is evolving out of the specific contradictions of the New World Order system, the tasks and challenges to governments are unique to this period. This is especially true in the U.S., which is holding onto an increasingly shaky and vulnerable leadership role over the entire global system.

With all of the domestic debate over the size and intrusiveness of the U.S. government both domestically and globally, it is important to keep in mind what the purpose of government is. *The fundamental purpose of government in any culture or in any political-economic system is to protect the system it serves.* When there are conflicting interests, the state steps in to resolve them to benefit the system as a whole. In a global capitalist system, the point of government is to protect capitalism as a system. In a constitutional democracy such as the United States, protection of the system defines the limits of all political debate.

In today's form of global capitalism, the system that the United States government protects is one in which it is presently the leader and a dominant force. As I have discussed earlier, today's New World Order is a global system in which production is located in the lowest cost areas of the world. And it is a system that is dominated by what I have termed "phantom markets" and "phantom products"—especially the trading of debt. This is what the U.S. Government and many other governments around the world are protecting.

The way government protects the present form of global capitalism—the New World Order—is first and foremost to represent the interests of the dominant players in the system. But the New World Order system has specific characteristics that make its protection particularly difficult. For one thing, the dominant players in the New World Order operate around the world and are not specifically tied to a single nation. Industrial firms operate in China, India, Korea, Vietnam or wherever they can extract the most value. Resources needed for production are also extracted all over the world. The lifeblood of the system—the buying and selling of debt in the form of derivatives—is also a global operation, as these phantom products are traded in exchanges around the world.

Over the past 20 years, the U.S. Government has facilitated the global movement and operations of capitalist enterprise even when it has meant unemployment or lower wages for its own residents. This has given rise to some contentious politics within the U.S. We are also seeing political conflict in other nations that have attempted to protect the interests of the system over domestic concerns. The conflicts in nations such as Greece, Spain, France, England and Germany are examples. The interests of global capitalist enterprise have trumped domestic considerations every time. And now that the New World Order system is in crisis, the task of representing the system as a whole is much more difficult. It involves conflicts between various players in the system as well as conflicts between system-wide needs and the needs of the residents of nations who depend on domestic governance.

Some have argued that as capitalist enterprise has become more global, national governments have become increasingly less effective. This is true to a degree. But the decline of the ability of the governments of nations to represent global capitalism's interests while attending to the needs of their own residents has been greater in some nations than in others. Many of the less developed nations have lost considerable autonomy through penetration of their national economies by transnational corporations through trade agreements and conditions placed on loans needed for development. And the governments of the more developed nations, especially the U.S., have found it exceeding difficult to protect the system as a whole while meeting domestic needs. However, the assessment that the power of nation states has declined to the extent of being "hollow states" with little if any power is overstated.

National governments continue to have a vital role to play by facilitating the movement and functioning of capital around the world. They protect global capitalist enterprise from hostile movements or governments that attempt to operate outside of the system. And governments placate or oppress peoples within their own borders who are adversely affected by the workings of the global system. The capitalist system cannot function unless the working classes within each nation can reproduce themselves and help to reproduce the system as a whole. While the U.S. government finds its position as the dominant leader of the system increasingly challenged, it is still a major player in the New World Order. Its role is comparable to that once played by leaders of empires of past ages. The most obvious is its military role.

The New World Order needs order and the U.S. is the dominant military force in the world. In addition to the use of its military, the U.S., as the current leader of global capitalism, also has a specific economic role to play that involves facilitating the global operations of industry and phantom derivatives trading. This is why the U.S. has been a leader in creating so called "trade agreements" such as the World Trade Organization that undermine the sovereignty of other nations, but enable the New World Order to work and reproduce itself.

But as the present *crisis of value* deepens, national governments, including the U.S. government, face difficult challenges. For one thing, national government revenues all ultimately come from income. Therefore government spending represents a claim on value. The New World Order, which provided a twenty-five year reprieve from the previous crisis of the 1970s, was designed to reduce labor's share of the value they produced. One result of this attack on labor was lowered revenues available to government at all levels. As U.S. factories closed, the loss of living wage jobs not only meant misery for the thousands of victims of the transition to the New World Order, but a loss of revenue to governments at all levels. Local school systems, municipalities, state governments and the Federal Government experienced a drop in revenues relative to the price of and demand for services. Yet citizens continued to insist on quality schools, police and fire protection, public transportation, highway maintenance, and Medicare and Medicaid payments. Those victimized by New World Order jobs destruction also continued to demand a social safety net that included unemployment benefits, housing subsidies, food stamps, and public welfare support.

For the U.S. Federal Government, the revenue/expenditure deficit was even greater due to defense and "homeland security" costs which presently consume about 60% of each year's Federal budget. Although the New World Order strategy of lowering labor's share of global value did indeed lower revenues at a federal level, there was a relatively easy (albeit unsustainable) solution. Because the U. S. dollar is the global reserve currency (all nations do business with each other in dollars), and because the U.S. is as politicians love to say, "the most powerful nation in the world," there was a seemingly endless demand for U.S. Government bonds.

Bonds backed by the U.S. government were, and still are, considered to be the safest investment in the world. That means the U.S. Government, can borrow and print money to avoid financial shortfalls. So, annual deficits in the federal budget continue and the size of the national debt (the accumulation of annual deficits) continues to rise. Earlier I pointed out that the size of the U.S. national debt relative to the size of the economy is not especially great compared to other nations in the world. But there are troubling questions about the continued viability of the ongoing practice of deficit spending. If the U.S. economy continues to generate greater claims on value than it is producing, there could be a sharp decline, or even collapse, of the demand for dollars and U.S. debt. Also, if other nations or coalitions of nations challenge the reign of the dollar as the global reserve currency, the U.S. Government might have a very difficult time borrowing to make up deficits. Printing dollars without global demand could lead to seriously high levels of inflation.

Many of the political struggles and divisions in Washington are related to the contradiction between: a. the need of the U.S. government to manage the entire global system while maintaining politically needed expenditures at home, and b. the economic need of the system to keep labor's share of value reduced. The contradiction has appeared in a number of forms. An important one is the ongoing struggle over income distribution. This struggle was most recently manifested during the presidential elections in the dispute over whether to retain President Bush's tax cuts for the wealthy (people earning over $250,000 a year), and during the "fiscal cliff" and "sequester" debates before and after the elections. *But these debates do not begin to address the real reason the rich have become richer and the poor, poorer beginning in the 1980s. The real explanation is the systemic need to lower labor's share of global value.* And that ongoing need of the capitalist system is not even on the table for discussion.

The government's need to protect the system places limits on any move to achieve a more equal distribution of income. If political discussion in the U.S. did debate the viability of the system, it would become clear that labor's reduced share of value is one pole of a contradiction. As this contradiction appears with greater and greater force, government policy, attempting to protect the current system of value production and distribution, actually contributes to the crisis of value by increasing claims on value without producing value itself. National government thus becomes a key contributor to the self-destruction of the New World Order.

The fiscal crises that state and local governments find themselves in are a different matter. States and localities do not have the ability to simply print money, and they are required by law to balance their budgets each year. Nor is there an automatic market for their bonds that the Federal Government enjoys. Revenue bonds may be sold for specific projects that can be paid off from project revenues, such as tolls on highways. General obligation bonds, backed by the "full faith and credit" of whatever government is selling them, can be sold as well. But too much borrowing will ultimately result in lower credit ratings on these bonds, which means paying higher interest rates and/or greater difficulty in selling state and local bonds.

As factories closed and incomes fell for large segments of the U.S. population, governments dependent on property taxes and income taxes—municipalities, school districts, state governments—began to feel the pinch. Raising property taxes or state income taxes was (and still is) increasingly burdensome on a population whose income had been devastated by factory closings that marked the beginning of a New World Order. Local services such as education, police and fire protection cannot easily be cut back.

Throughout the 1980s and 90s and into the new millennium, the fiscal crisis was contained, but it was a ticking time bomb that is now about to go off. To contain the fiscal crisis in state and local governments, clever politicians used a variety of tricks to postpose the day of reckoning until after these politicians were ready to retire. One trick was to raid the pension funds of public employees, including police officers, nurses, firemen and teachers. They accomplished this mainly by using funds earmarked for pensions to meet current government obligations. Another favorite was to privatize revenue-producing services by selling them to politically favored firms. In this way the government would get a huge injection of money by foregoing future revenues. The Mayor of Chicago, for example, sold the parking meters. The new private enterprise then increased parking fees, shifting local government costs to people who need parking spaces, in two ways. They forever deprived the city government of parking revenues, and made citizens pay more for this service without direct political responsibility. These and similar trickeries were repeated across the country.

As the present *crisis of value* began with the crash of housing derivatives markets and the subsequent collapse of housing prices, a full-blown fiscal crisis surfaced. At a federal level, a lack of economic growth has greatly lowered public revenues from income taxes at a time when wars are being fought with abandon. So we are running annual deficits and the size of the national debt rises both in absolute terms, and relative to economic growth. At the state and local level, the collapse of housing prices, reduced incomes and unemployment lowered both property tax revenues and state and local income taxes. State and local politicians then began to find ways to maintain public spending without large increases in tax rates on a population that is hurting from both a reduction of living-wage jobs and the collapse of the price (market "value") of their homes. One way politicians have attempted to deal with this contradiction has been to try to reduce public spending by attacking public employees, their pension and health care benefits, and their unions. They have also cut back services by closing and privatizing schools, reducing contributions to public higher education, decreasing the size of the police and fire departments and deferring maintenance of public infrastructure.

In Wisconsin, for example, conservative Republican Governor Scott Walker went after collective bargaining laws while attacking pay and benefits of teachers, nurses and other government employees. This generated a massive protest and recall campaign. The Governor was able to prevail in the recall referendum, but the issue continues to simmer. Meanwhile in Illinois, liberal Democratic Governor Pat Quinn and Chicago Public Schools Superintendent Arne Duncan (later President Obama's Education Secretary), joined forces with conservative business elites and the Democratic Party legislative leadership to undermine the power of the teachers' unions. They passed a law that would limit the right to strike strictly to issues of pay and benefits, leaving out issues like teacher evaluation, class size and distribution of resources in a school district. The law also required a 75% majority to call for a strike.

Then, both former Chicago Mayor Richard M. Daley and the present Mayor Rahm Emanuel (formerly President Obama's Chief of Staff) began to close schools. Emanuel followed this by canceling a scheduled 4% pay raise and lengthening the school day. In the new contract, the Mayor sought to minimize pay increases, tie evaluations to test scores and control teacher reassignments or dismissal in the event of layoffs. The teachers fought back with a strike backed by an unprecedented 90% vote of union members. They held massive public rallies. Their actions had solid support from most parents and fierce opposition from business groups and the local media. The teachers did win some concessions on pay and the basis for evaluation. But teachers and their supporters dubbed Mayor Emanuel "Scott Emanuel" as both Republican Governor Scott Walker and Republican Vice Presidential candidate Paul Ryan praised the Democratic Party mayor. Once the strike was over, the school board and the mayor announced the closing of 54 schools, which would affect 30,000 students and 1,000 teachers. The announcement of the closings sparked another massive protest.

The point is that the fiscal crisis that motivates both Republican and Democratic state and local politicians is an inherent feature of the New World Order itself. The crash of 2008-9 brought the federal, state and local government crisis to the surface, causing the fiscal chickens that had been hatching for more than two decades to come home to roost. But laying off public workers, raiding pension funds and cutting needed services raises unemployment and continues to undermine purchasing power that is needed for the New World Order system of capitalism to function. In this way state and local governments also contribute to the present *crisis of value* and the self-destruction of the New World Order. *The claims on value made through public expenditures cannot be met by the system. This is an important context of U.S. politics today.*

There are two key aspects of politics around today's fiscal crisis. First, politics at all levels of government in the U.S. is a struggle over who can lay the greater claim on available value. This struggle constitutes a conflict over shares of a pie that is increasingly inadequate to meet people's needs. Secondly, because of this, there is increased emphasis on issues that do not require politicians to propose policies that will need funding. This is why there is so much emphasis in the electoral political arena over the so-called cultural issues like abortion, gay marriage and prayer in the schools. As living standards of many people decline, there is a tendency to look for solace in religion and ethical questions linked to faith. Regardless of constitutional mandates to keep religion and politics separated, and the consequences for those whose choices or lifestyles may be negatively politicized, politicians use such issues to mobilize masses of people without having to confront the contradictions of government spending in the midst of a *crisis of value*. This also helps explain the rise in political appeals to American "exceptionalism" (more on that later) in the foreign policy arena, and an increase in U.S. residents' distrust and hostility toward other nations and cultures.

Furthermore, the rhetorical flourishes around "cultural" issues mask a real unity between the political parties and U.S. elites generally. The recent U.S. Presidential and Congressional elections presented the appearance of a politically divided nation.

Now that the elections are over, many people sincerely believe that the nation is headed for an unparalleled disaster, or that it has narrowly escaped one. Some of this is based on real differences over the "cultural" issues. But more broadly, the division is more apparent than real. Republicans have tried to argue that their vision of America is based on small government, low taxes, and business free of regulation. They attack the Democratic Party as being for big government, high taxes and interference with business and our personal lives (linking alleged government forays into social engineering to differences over these "cultural" issues).

The Democrats' response has been to move to the center of a very narrow political spectrum. They argue that the Republicans favor the rich, while their own policies help to build a "middle class" (undefined). Within this very narrow spectrum, there were differences over, 1) whose taxes should be cut the most, 2) whether the emission of greenhouse gasses should be uncontrolled or slightly regulated by creating a market for carbon credits, 3) the extent of regulation needed in the health insurance industry, and 4) whether or not government should use public funds to bail out failing banks and other businesses. And of course there was also the "Big Bird" question (when candidate Mitt Romney apologized to the public TV icon as he proposed to savage the public television budget).

The unspoken scope of agreement between and among candidates, however, suggests that U.S. political disagreement becomes a vehicle for removing far more fundamental issues from political discourse. Both parties wish to preserve the U.S. position as the center of global economic and military power, which has been in place since the 1946 Bretton Woods Agreement at the end of World War II. Both parties want to preserve the New World Order system that has been in place since the 1980s, and has been supported by Presidents Carter, Reagan, Bush, Clinton, Bush and Obama. Both parties wish to use a combination of diplomacy and militarism to protect U.S. power and the New World Order programs throughout the world. *By holding onto a system that has generated greater claims on value than the system can produce, both political parties are taking stances that contribute to the self destruction of the New World Order system. Ironically, they will continue to do so because they are committed to the preservation of the system as it is.* Within U.S. politics today, whether the programs and policies of either party can accomplish what they aim to seems beside the point!

The contradiction between government's need to hold onto a system in crisis by acting in ways that contribute to that crisis highlights the importance of the point I made at the beginning of this section: Government in any kind of society is organized to protect the prevailing system.

The present system in the U.S. and much of the world is one where, 1) the U.S. is "the most powerful nation in the world," 2) purchasing power depends on debt being a tradable commodity, and 3) profit rates depend on producing value without adequately compensating the producers. The U.S. Government's policies and politics will attempt to keep these three elements in place no matter which political party is in power. The entire U.S. political system, including state and local governments, is designed to keep its democracy within the confines of these three elements. "Legitimate" and "practical" political discourse and all electoral debate is limited to how best to maintain the present system. For most people in the U.S. these three elements have become "mind-forged manacles."

I will further develop these points by going into detail in four areas of American government and politics: a) the reconstruction of "common sense", b) elections, c) economic policy, and d) militarism.

a. The Reconstruction of "Common Sense"

Any established economic-political-social system requires wide scale cooperation on the part of ordinary people. Cooperation requires agreement on a variety of notions about how the world works. This requirement can be conceptualized as simply "common sense."

Back in 1776, the British-born American revolutionary Thomas Payne wrote a pamphlet called *Common Sense*, which attacked the widespread notion that the peoples in the American colonies needed the British monarchy in order to improve themselves and prosper. Payne's pamphlet is considered one of the best selling and most widely read books in history—around a half million copies were sold to a population of about 2 million. Many heard it read in taverns and on street corners. At the beginning of the pamphlet, Payne wrote: "A long habit of not thinking a thing WRONG gives it a superficial appearance of being RIGHT, and raises at first a formidable outcry in defense of custom." He went on to demonstrate the contradictory aspects of the notion of monarchy and reconciliation with England, as well as other aspects of prevailing common sense that later became enshrined in the Declaration of Independence as the right to "life, liberty and the pursuit of happiness." The ongoing war with England, the reconstruction of common sense led by Paine, and the Declaration of Independence broke the hold of the British Crown on the American peoples. The need for monarchy was eliminated from the prevailing conception of common sense in the British colonies of America.

In the 1930's Italian philosopher and revolutionary Antonio Gramsci also employed the term "common sense" to discuss the importance of ideas in waging a social revolution. (These references to Gramsci come from his *Prison Notebooks* written around 1932. They can be found in English in *An Antonio Gramsci Reader: Selected Writings 1916-35,* David Forcacs (1988) Schocken Books.) Gramsci opposed Italian Fascism; in fact these ideas were written from prison where he ultimately died at the hands of Mussolini and his fascist party. His notion was that a common sense based worldview consists of a number of diffuse, uncoordinated and often contradictory features that include aspects of language, religion, superstitions, opinions, and ways of seeing things and living our lives. Any bundle of these features is specific to a particular period or even social movement. For this reason, Gramsci argued that a reconstruction of common sense is always needed as a basis for major systemic change. And such a reconstruction needs to highlight contradictory elements within prevailing common sense, using the resolution of contradictions in thought to create something new.

A reconstruction of common sense has not been limited to periods of social revolution. *In the entire history of capitalism, whenever crisis has forced a major reconstruction of the system, there have been parallel reconstructions of "common sense."* Such reconstruction has drawn on elements of existing common sense as well as on oppositional theories and philosophies that had been languishing on the edges of society for some time. In these cases intellectual elites and political leaders highlight contradictions between prevailing common sense and the emerging new system. This was true of the crisis and restructuring that occurred between 1920 and 1945. Government and social elites played a decisive role in shaping the "common sense" that evolved. Their motivation was to protect the essence of the capitalist system as it evolved during the Great Depression through Roosevelt's New Deal and later, after World War II, in the form of the Bretton Woods system that I described. They needed a political atmosphere that would ensure cooperation with the new system. For this reason, ideas from social movements that called for social change were taken wholesale from opposing movements in order to bring them into the political mainstream.

In the 1920s and 1930s, for example, an insurgent labor movement and other organizations representing those suffering during the Great Depression demanded a political and economic response. Later, in the late 1950s and through the 1960s, Blacks, Latinos, American Indians and women also made their voices heard during a wave of Civil Rights movements. Many of their demands and ideas were adapted to reorganize the existing order, reconstructing prevailing common sense and bringing formerly opposing groups to the center of American politics in the 1970s.

There are many elements of the common sense that prevailed during these periods. I will highlight just a few of them below. But the general point is that the philosophical and theoretical ideas behind these elements were already dormant in society and in the minds and activities of scholars, activists and politicians as well as the masses of people. *It was the convergence of practical activity, ideas, and material conditions of society that resulted in a reconstruction of common sense.*

The key ideas that evolved through two periods of crisis from the 1920s through the 1960s included a heightened sense of the importance of the social dimension of everyday life. People viewed themselves as part of one or more groups—a social class, a racial or ethnic group, gender, residential community or workplace. The importance of these social dimensions of life was easily channeled into a political mainstream that fit the New Deal, mobilization during World War II, and the post war Bretton Woods system. Trade union activity and the Democratic Party became a key outlet for class identity. Compromises on civil rights demands through national legislation became a focus of social justice groupings. Not-for-profit corporations and foundations fit their missions to the needs of specific groups and communities that were considered "disadvantaged."

The evolving emphasis on social being also suggested a strong role for government to meet social needs within the confines of Bretton Woods-era capitalism. This included the implementation of safety net programs beginning with the New Deal and extending to such things as public housing, welfare, Social Security, food stamps, Medicare, and expanded public education. It also involved a strong hand for government in running the economy including both the regulation of business and the use of taxing and spending authority to stabilize the economy, offsetting periods of inflation and unemployment. Also, the government, through its Federal Reserve Banking system, controlled the supply of money, which also influenced prices and employment levels. Often this was done through the practice of deficit spending that resulted in a public debt.

The center of U.S. politics questioned none of this through most of the period between 1945 and the early 1970s. The idea that government could use its taxing and spending powers to meet social needs was part of the broad common sense. There was a strong theoretical justification for all of this. Key was the economic theories of John Maynard Keynes, whose book *The General Theory of Employment, Interest and Money* was dominant in universities, government and politics throughout the period. There were a variety of other social science theories and ideas that dominated educational institutions during this time that reinforced and shaped the center of American politics, and became a part of prevailing common sense.

One aspect of common sense is the idea of "American Exceptionalism." This notion has been central to U.S. politics for the past 236 years of U.S. history. As a conservative commentator wrote recently in *National Review*, American Exceptionalism is "recognition that America is, as James Madison said, the 'hope of liberty throughout the world' and that America is different from other nations in ways that are consequential for the world." (*National Review Online*, November 1, 2011.) This is not a conservative idea, but a uniquely American idea. During the Bretton Woods period it was utilized to channel group antagonisms that had surfaced during the Great Depression and the Civil Rights movements into support for the American system. This included U.S. foreign policy, which was focused on opposition to the Soviet Union's global influence in the developing world. It also spilled over into a strong strain of anti-communism at home. American Exceptionalism, anti-communism, and the Cold War with the Soviet Union defined the center of American politics and established the boundaries of the social dimensions of domestic policy and even social movements.

The Bretton Woods system began to unravel in the 1960s, which unleashed a challenge to both the prevailing common sense and government policies. The *crisis of value* that surfaced in the mid 1970s and the economic restructuring that developed into the 1980s and 1990s required massive reconstruction of the common sense that had defined the Bretton Woods era. The emphasis on the social dimension of everyday life contradicted the new reality that included factory closings and loss of living wage jobs, simultaneous double-digit inflation and double-digit unemployment, and a fiscal crisis in which government could no longer finance the previous era's extensive social safety net programs.

Beginning with the Reagan Administration in 1981, the individualization of everyday life was the main feature of the reconstruction of common sense. This feature contradicted American politics and policies that stressed the social dimension. That common sense notion was challenged by an alternative: the pursuit of a decent life could no longer come through your class, race, gender or nationality but through individuals making good choices and working hard to achieve their goals. This challenge gained force as the economic crisis deepened and the old policy medicine no longer worked. As factories closed and eliminated living wage jobs, advancement that enabled minorities and women to gain living wage jobs as part of a social class or through government mandated affirmative action was no longer feasible. Policies that had established a social safety net such as public housing, welfare and affordable higher education meant higher taxes to a population that was losing living wage jobs and had higher levels of debt. Government was no longer seen as part of the solution. Common sense was found wanting and the people of the U.S. were open to its reconstruction.

The reconstruction did not come out of thin air. As the Bretton Woods system unraveled, both the social dimension of everyday life and individualism, and a repudiation of "big government" were firmly in place as contradictory elements of American common sense. The ascendancy of individualism was at the heart of this reconstruction. In addition, two lines of thought—both consistent with a rising individualism—merged to replace an "outmoded" common sense grounded in group identity. Often termed neoliberalism and neoconservatism today, they had been developing at the fringes of American thought since the 1940s.

Neoliberalism was initiated by a number of economists who believed that private businesses operating in "free" (without government regulation or control) and competitive markets would produce optimal results for the economy and for the individuals and businesses that live and work in it. This notion was contrary to both New Deal programs and those of economist John Maynard Keynes, who prescribed a proactive role for government in running the economy. Neoliberalism asserted to the contrary, that competitive markets, unregulated by government, sent the signals needed by both firms and individuals to make rational choices and decisions. The result would be the greatest efficiency (lowest cost per item produced) possible. Greater efficiency would mean greater jobs and income. Government's only legitimate role in guiding the economy was to use its power to control the supply of money, a theory known as monetarism. (A good source of the history of neoliberalism is David Harvey's *Brief History of Neoliberalism*.)

Among the chief architects of this theory were "Austrian School" economists Friedrich Von Hayek and Ludwig Von Mises, and University of Chicago economist Milton Friedman. In 1947, they formed what they called the Mont Pelerin Society, consisting of other economists and wealthy businessmen. Their aim was to defeat the ideas of Keynes, his followers, and the government policies that flowed from those ideas. They met regularly for the next thirty years producing theoretical papers, founding think tanks, taking over academic and popular journals, placing their people in key government posts, producing textbooks and ultimately dominating graduate schools of economics. They even successfully implemented their theories on an experimental basis through their influence over General Pinochet and his military junta, which in 1973 overthrew a popularly elected government in Chile.

The founders of neoconservatism included a group of philosophers, social scientists, disillusioned communists and traditional conservatives. Many took part in intense discussions at City Colleges of New York (CCNY) during the late 1930s and throughout the 1940s. (Some sources on these developments include: Irving Kristol, *Neo-conservatism: The Autobiography of an Idea*; Francis Fukuyama, *America at the Crossroads*; Alice O'Connor, *Poverty Knowledge*.) The development of the ideas that today constitute neoconservatism began with agreement on the centrality of American Exceptionalism (discussed earlier). The founders of these ideas also shared a profound distrust of government programs that were geared toward influencing the behavior of its citizens. In short, they were against "social engineering."

The CCNY neoconservative pioneers also started think tanks and journals like *Partisan Review* (that began as a communist publication), *Commentary* and *Public Inte*rest. As their ideas developed they became well placed in academia and politics. These ideas also influenced another strain of neoconservatism that came out of debates over the nature of poverty; the origins of this strain go back to the turn of the 20th century at the University of Chicago. Alice O'Connor's excellent study, *Poverty Knowledge*, covers this in depth. Fundamental to the evolving neoconservative view of poverty was that it was the product, in O'Connor's words, of "individual failings rather than structural inequality, of cultural and skill 'deficits' rather than unequal distribution of power and wealth..."

Similarly to neoliberalism, the ideas that originated with CCNY intellectuals and University of Chicago poverty theorists developed outside of the prevailing common sense of the Bretton Woods period. During that period, the debate over the nature of poverty raged between those who emphasized structural inequality, and those who saw poverty as an individual failing. And CCNY intellectuals debated about how Bretton Woods era policies departed from notions of American Exceptionalism and promoted social engineering. Ultimately, these ideas fused with neoliberalism in the mid 1970s. The post World War II Bretton Woods/New Deal system had been undermined by closed factories and falling incomes for the working class. Something new was needed both politically and in terms of economic and social policy. The fusion of the two strains of ideas that had been percolating for nearly fifty years filled the void.

The process of fusion that resulted in a reconstructed common sense is varied and complex. Here I will only hit the highlights.

The University of Chicago became a key center of neoliberal thought. Milton Friedman, and later Gary Becker and Robert Lucas, expanded the applications of the Mont Pelerin Society's original ideas. Friedman developed the theories of "rational expectations" and "rational choices," initially by arguing that government policies that pushed for full employment were futile. This, he said, was because individual business leaders, anticipating inflation, would raise prices and individual workers anticipating higher prices would demand higher wages.

A decade later, Robert Lucas used a "rational choice" framework to contend that all economics was based on the behavior of individual firms and consumers. This ruled out any positive role for a national government creating policies that benefited the economic system as a whole. His theory contradicted the ideas of Keynesian economics that dominated government policies and programs. Gary Becker used the rational choice and rational expectations theories to extend economics to the fields of sociology and political science. He applied economic analysis to human behaviors that encompassed racial discrimination, crime, drug addiction, and worker employability and earning potential. All three of these theorists gained international recognition when they received Nobel Memorial Prizes in 1976, 1992 and 1995.

The expanded ideas and influence of the Mont Pelerin Society were a perfect complement to the neoconservative distrust of government social engineering, and also provided a rallying point in the poverty debate. Seeing human behavior in terms of market choices meant that poverty and even racial discrimination were the consequence of individual failings—poor choices made worse by government meddling. These ideas also provided political

116

justification for the evolving reconstruction of the Bretton Woods-era capitalist system, where closing factories could be explained in terms of rational choices in a New World Order. Social programs that constituted a demand on value could be gutted with the argument that they actually *contributed* to poverty. Poverty was blamed on individual failures that had resulted in a "tangle of pathologies in the inner city," including violent crime, mother-only households, welfare dependency, out of wedlock births, teenage pregnancies and joblessness.

Philanthropic foundations like Rockefeller and Ford fueled the emerging common sense about poverty, economics and government. While at the University of Chicago key sociological researcher, William Julius Wilson, developed a whole theory of the "underclass" that built upon the work of neoconservatives and gave it a "liberal" stamp. He became a key advisor to President Clinton.

The Clinton Administration did more than either Ronald Reagan or George H.W. Bush to institute the global New World Order, consolidating both a reconstructed capitalist system and a reconstructed common sense. President Clinton gutted public welfare and public housing programs, largely privatizing the latter by offering subsidy vouchers instead of homes to the poorest citizens. Private "charter schools" were created to solve failing public education. His administration significantly deregulated the finance industry making possible the phantom markets that were critical to the New World Order. He also made it possible for U.S. industrial and finance capital to roam the world, by negotiating and implementing treaties such as the World Trade Organization and the North American Free Trade Agreement.

Finally, the exercise of American Exceptionalism was greatly expanded through President George W. Bush's response to the attack on the World Trade Center in 2001. Bush instituted a policy of preventive war by attacking Iraq and Afghanistan, claiming he was bringing liberty and democracy to the entire world. The Obama Administration quickly fell into line with all of its predecessors since Reagan.

The reconstructed common sense makes it imperative that American politics maintain the U.S. as the "most powerful nation in the world." The common sense that markets and individual initiative are the basis of all progress is seen as the basis for this power. While the size of government debt is presently being challenged, along with the excesses of the finance industry that brought financial collapse to the nation, the basic system that depends on debt remains firmly intact. Meanwhile, a system in which profit rates depend on the exploitation of labor goes unchallenged.

b. U.S. Elections as Thought Control

U.S. elections have evolved as a vehicle to keep American common sense intact and unchallenged. A system of perpetual and increasingly expensive elections, two dominant parties that have programs well within the range of the New World Order system, and a media that channels all political discourse into the confines of electoral issues combine to eliminate any serious challenge to the system itself. As a result, elections, far from being an exercise of democracy, are a form of thought control.

The U.S. system of perpetual elections makes it difficult to engage in a political process outside of elections. No sooner had Barack Obama been elected president in 2008, than the Republican

Party began lining up candidates and issues to take back Congress and the various state governments. And once those elections were completed, the Republican Party presidential primary campaigns began. Those went on for nearly two years. When President Obama was elected for a second term, the cycle of lining up candidates for another round of elections began to repeat itself. Depending on which state you live in, you could have been subjected to a barrage of campaign ads and information-free news coverage of national elections for four solid years! When you consider state and local offices, the perpetual electoral process is even more all-consuming.

These elections are increasingly expensive, which rules out candidates who lack access to lots of money. Also, it is difficult to determine exactly how much money has been spent on all election campaigns over any period of time. This is especially difficult when local and statewide elections are considered, though organizations that keep track of electoral spending, like the Center for Responsive Politics, contend that new spending records are set every election year.

In the 2008 presidential election year, $5.3 billion was spent for all national elections. The presidential race alone spent $2.4 billion. The 2012 national November elections cost over $6 billion. $2.6 billion was spent on the presidential campaign. (Data from the Center for Responsive Politics blog: www.OpenSecrets.org). Candidates not only have to raise campaign money, they have to take positions that attract outside money from political action committees that operate outside of campaign committees. Some of this money includes "shadow funds," to be spent on "non political" ads appearing outside of the context of the campaigns themselves. An example would be the flurry of "clean coal" ads during the 2012 presidential campaign.

Excluding PAC and shadow monies, the average incumbent Senator raised $11 million for reelection over a six-year term. Candidates seeking an open Senate seat raised on average $2.5 million. The comparable numbers for seats in the House of Representatives are $1.5 million and $453,000 respectively. Outside money that is not formally part of a campaign adds greatly to spending. Candidates don't directly raise this money, but they do have to take positions on issues that will insure spending on advertising favorable to their campaign. It is impossible to even estimate the amount of so-called shadow money, but most other outside funds come through the Political Action Committees.

In 2010, the Supreme Court case known as Citizens United opened the floodgates for outside spending by legalizing "Super PACs." It is now possible for anonymous individual donors to spend an unlimited amount of money supporting specific candidates. Some of these individuals readily admit they are spending millions of dollars to fund electoral campaigns. This year, wealthy businessman Harold Simmons donated $12 million to the Super PAC "American Crossroads," controlled by conservative political operative, Karl Rove. Bob Perry, a billionaire homebuilder from Houston, Texas, donated about $2.5 million to Rove's Super PAC. Industrialists David and Charles Koch bankroll another Super PAC/political organization: Americans for Prosperity. They, along with former House Speaker Richard Armey, who controls the Super PAC called Freedom Works, have funded the Tea Party Movement that has run people for office against more moderate Republicans. They have influenced the

Republican Party stances on a number of issues. Despite the fact that these Super PACs lost the presidential election as well as a number of key congressional and local elections, they forced more moderate Republican candidates and Democratic Party, or "liberal" candidates, into a political middle within the American common sense. And they set a standard for the cost of elections.

The increasingly expensive electoral process makes it nearly impossible for an individual to make a credible run for national, or even statewide office outside the two party system. Nor is it likely that a separate party can muster the funds needed to seriously contend for public office.

The legislative gridlock in Washington and the increasingly contentious political rhetoric between Republican and Democratic Parties give the appearance of a sharp political divide. It seems that every time I have expressed negative feelings about Obama to my liberal friends they have exclaimed, "But consider the alternative!" When Obama won, a number of conservatives I know seemed to go into deep depression and expressed the view that "the country is really in big trouble now!"

The differences between Republicans and Democrats in the past decade have really boiled down to two areas. One is the very real "cultural" difference over such things as same sex marriage, equal treatment for homosexuals, affirmative action and abortion. The other has to do with who is to bear the burden of the deepening crisis of value. Democrats want the wealthy (individuals earning more than $200,000 per year) to pay more income taxes and the "middle class" to pay less. The issue of "entitlement spending" is in the same category. Which spending cuts will be made and how much? There was no consideration of poverty in either party platform or by major political candidates. And there are no differences over policies and actions designed to keep the U.S. as "the most powerful nation in the world," which it has been since the end of World War II and the Bretton Woods agreement. There are no differences over the use of debt to enhance purchasing power or over the subsequent treatment of debt as a commodity. There is no difference over maintaining labor's reduced claims on value. There was no questioning of the common sense proposition that progress comes through individual effort. Both parties continued to ignore any social dimension in everyday life. In short, even as they bickered furiously over the specifics of how to keep the present form of capitalism intact in the wake of the crisis of value, neither the political parties nor any individual candidates challenged the proposition that our system should be preserved. In fact there was, within the perpetual electoral cycle, a remarkable unity over the most fundamental propositions of the broad political center that make up American common sense.

This unity was only reinforced by the media, which raked in billions of dollars for political ads. The political news consisted mainly of various approval ratings, polls in "battleground" states and snippets from speeches by one candidate or the other. The parties themselves controlled the format and participation criteria of presidential debates. Parties or candidates operating outside the two party framework were universally ignored. Even right wing libertarian and tea party favorite Ron Paul was dismissed as outside the mainstream. Political commentators on the major television networks limited their comments to the topics raised by the mainstream candidates and their parties.

Because elections were basically about who could best maintain the present system, and because the electoral cycles suck up nearly all civic political discussion, they are a form of thought control. It seems to most citizens that their only option is to go with the electoral flow. Given the fact that there exists a political center that reflects today's reconstructed common sense, it is not surprising that government policy cannot stray from that center. In this time of an economic *crisis of value*, this state of affairs is reflected in economic policy.

c. Economic Policy

Economic policy, like the electoral system, is designed to protect and sustain an economic and social system in which the U.S. is "the most powerful nation in the world," where purchasing power depends on debt being a tradable commodity, and where profit rates depend on producing value without adequately compensating the producers of value. Politically, there is no credible challenge to any of these three elements. Yet, the system is in crisis. It depends on debt. Without sufficient production of value, mounting government, corporate and household debt is not sustainable. Dependence on debt without sufficient value production to pay it off is a contradiction. U.S. economic policies, by seeking to preserve the new world order, can only heighten this contradiction further.

When I was in graduate school (in 1963!), my courses in economic theory and economic policy taught the prevailing common sense notion that government had a critical role to play in guiding the economy. An economist named Richard Musgrave was enjoying considerable popularity. He argued that government economic policy should do three kinds of things:

allocate resources of nations in desirable directions, redistribute income, and stabilize the economy when there was too much unemployment or rapidly rising prices.

1. Resource Allocation: There were, Musgrave argued, certain social needs like police and fire protection, national defense, building and maintaining transportation routes, and education. They were social needs because once they were provided to society no one could be excluded from the benefits, therefore we all had to share in their costs. A second reason for government to allocate resources from government revenues he called merit needs. These included things like education, health care, housing, food, and public welfare that we, as a people, have decided everyone needs.

The period after World War II saw a rise in public spending for both social and merit needs, including education, public housing, public welfare, health care and education. But since the 1980s, as the global capitalist system reorganized itself into a New World Order, spending on social and merit needs has undergone a shift. As I emphasized earlier, the New World Order reduced labor's share of value and substituted debt for wages by turning debt into a commodity to be bought and sold. As a result, the political power of the finance sector rose. This had an impact on economic policy in two ways.

First, because rising prices threatened the money value of dollar denominated assets, including government bonds and real estate, keeping inflation as low as possible (even at the expense of unemployment) became the priority of government economic policy. Secondly, governmental taxing and spending policies emphasized individual choice rather than meeting social and merit needs.

These two policy impacts, however, contained a contradiction that we are still grappling with as the present *crisis of value* deepens. As factory closings meant that workers began to lose living wage jobs, tax revenues based on income decreased. Yet the need for spending on merit and social wants like public assistance (welfare), public housing, health care, education, and food subsidies increased. Also, the expansion of New World Order programs around the world gave rise to a series of wars, which increased military expenditures.

This contradiction had a number of different kinds of impacts on economic policy. One impact was a dramatic rise of government debt. Between 1981 and 1989, under President Reagan, gross public debt (the sum of federal, state and local government debt) increased from under 45% of gross domestic product to over 60%. Since then, the federal government's portion of that debt relative to state and local debt, has increased and constitutes the bulk of public debt. Federal government debt came down a bit during President Clinton's administration. But beginning with the Bush Administration in 2001, debt has been consistently rising as a percentage of GDP.

As I write this (2013), federal government debt is about 108% of GDP. This is a lot (in money terms: $16.4 trillion), but not as high as other nations, and not even the highest in history—in 1945 U.S. public debt was 122% of GDP. But debt has a contradictory character as the *crisis of value* deepens. Debt is needed, but the continuing growth of debt in the absence of economic growth could bring about inflation, which especially concerns the financiers. As a result, mainstream politicians have agreed that we need to bring down the debt; this is why Congress and the President agreed to set a deadline for bringing it under control.

Without a balanced budget for 2013, there would be automatic spending cuts in all categories, called "sequestration." Congress, the White House and the media have not questioned the wisdom of trying to balance the budget during a period of crisis. Never in our history has there been so much concern about public debt. Today's debt politics are the result of the contradictory impacts of the New World Order system in crisis. And government economic policy is a prime example of churning and flailing that goes with a *crisis of value.*

There has been another kind of shift in the government's efforts to meet rising social and merit needs in the context of New World Order common sense. First, the very notion of social and merit needs contradicts the New World Order common sense notion of the individualization of everyday life. Yet the needs are there, stimulated by the success of the New World Order program of lowering labor's share of value. Those needs become even greater as the New World Order system plunges into crisis. Since 1960, there has actually been a steady rise in Federal Government expenditures as a percentage of GDP for the broad categories of health, education and welfare. The shift has not been in the total amount spent but in the nature of many government social programs. Government benefits for education, and welfare (including housing) have been individualized and to a degree have shifted away from an emphasis on the poor. Housing is a prime example.

During the Clinton Administration, public housing—where the government owns, manages and subsidizes rents of poor people—has all but been replaced by vouchers that poor people can use to try to find private rental housing. Public housing itself has either been torn down or economically integrated, encouraging a mix of tenants where rent levels vary with income. This has amounted to the privatization of housing subsidies for the poor. Furthermore, since 2004, Federal expenditures for public housing and vouchers have declined slightly, while tax deductions or tax reductions for housing have increased. They are now three and a half times greater than the declining spending outlays. Such tax breaks mainly include the tax deduction for mortgage interest payments and capital gains exclusions on home sales. This amounts to shifting social and merit need resource allocation from the very poor to the "middle class" and the wealthy.

2. Income Distribution: My graduate economics courses (that featured the framework of economist Richard Musgrave), argued that government should also use its powers to tax and spend to achieve an agreed upon distribution of income. Higher tax rates for the rich would make income distribution more equal. Expenditures for things like public housing and food stamps would effectively transfer some income from the society as a whole to the poor. In the post World War II/Bretton Woods period, it was U.S. government policy to make income distribution more equal in order to quell rising social rebellion and to enable working people to buy more consumer goods. The Post World War II private sector also agreed to give labor a greater share of the windfall brought about by the post war industrialization, which also contributed to a more equal distribution of income.

One commonly used measure of income equality is called the "GINI index." Using this measure, perfect income equality would be zero—everyone in the economy has the same proportion of the total income. Perfect income inequality, in which one person has all the income, is 1. The GINI index in the U.S. is approximately .46 at this time. We are, in fact, among the nations with the highest degree of inequality. We are not nearly as bad as South Africa where the number is about .70, but are far more unequal than Sweden and Norway, who are below .25. Most importantly, our society has become more unequal over time. In 1947—the beginning of the Post World War II/Bretton Woods period—the GINI index for the U.S. stood at about .41. Into the 1970s, the index fell steadily, meaning we became more equal. In 1967, the index was .39. In 1968 it was .38 and .39 again in 1970. But by the year 2000 it had risen to .46, where it stands today. (www.data.wordbank.org/indicator/SLPOVGINI)

Government policy is not the only reason for growing income inequality in the U.S. Greater income inequality is a measure of the success of the New World Order goal of reducing labor's share of value. Shipping the living wage jobs of the industrial sector around the world was one way this was accomplished. Another was for executives to take a greater and greater share of total income as salaries and bonuses. (Check out the annual report by The Institute for Policy Studies on "Executive Excess: www.ips-dc/reports/executive-excess-2013) The attack on organized labor, increasingly condoned by governments at all levels, is a factor as well.

Government economic policy has also played an important role in making the distribution of income more unequal. The present array of tax loopholes and deductions is one testament to this; tax cuts for the wealthy under Presidents Reagan and Bush is another. However, the impact of government policy on income distribution is not only through taxes. Deregulation of the finance sector and government participation in encouraging the trade of debt as a commodity have made huge income gains possible for the wealthy. Also, the distribution impact of U.S. "trade" policy is often overlooked. Such policy includes the rules of the International Monetary Fund, the World Trade Organization and agreements like the North American Free Trade Agreement. These policies opened up the economies of other nations to U.S. investment, and contributed greatly to the mobility that closed down factories in the U.S. Therefore, they also indirectly contributed to the growth of income inequality.

3. Stabilization: I was taught in the 1960s that stabilization is the third function of government economic policy. The idea was that at times of unemployment and recession, government could use its economic policy tools to stimulate the economy. The main tools stressed at that time were spending and taxing. Such policy was in line with the ideas of economist John Maynard Keynes. Government should, according to this view, increase spending and cut taxes during a recession even if it means more debt. "Deficit financing" was a policy right in line with the common sense of the time. In an inflationary period it was felt the opposite should be done—government should decrease spending and increase taxes.

Mainstream politicians and policy makers accepted this approach until, in the late 1970s, we experienced a *crisis of value* that simultaneously took the form of high unemployment and high inflation. The Mont Pelerin Society's ideas were waiting in the wings. In line with these ideas, the Federal Government went after inflation, allowing unemployment to soar. They then began a regime of austerity that has now achieved the status of common sense in the U.S. and around the world. The tools of choice, however, were no longer confined mainly to taxing and spending, but emphasized altering the supply of money through the Federal Reserve Banking system while cutting spending. During the 1980s and 1990s, whenever there was even a hint of inflation, money supply was lowered and spending decreased, increasing what the Mont Pelerin economists called a "natural rate of unemployment."

4. The Special Role of the Federal Reserve Bank System: There is one more subject I need to discuss under economic policy. Earlier I talked about changing the supply of money and altering interest rates as an economic policy tool that was initially emphasized by the Mont Pelerin Society and which inspires the economic and political mainstream today. Basically, when inflation threatens, the supply of money is decreased. When there is unemployment and a low economic growth rate, more money is put into circulation. The U.S. institution that can alter the supply of money is the Federal Reserve Banking system: the FED.

The FED controls the entire U.S. banking system. It accomplishes this by regulating the activities of the more than ten thousand member banks. Among its powers, it can establish the amount of deposits each bank must keep on hand. It controls key interest rates. The FED is also a "lender of the last resort"—it can lend money to the government, banks and financial institutions in times of emergency. This function was exercised during the 2008 collapse. The FED can also buy government debt, a power it has employed in the past several years, which has the effect of circulating more money in the economy. Through such activities, the FED effectively controls the supply of money. This "monetary policy" aspect of FED work impacts the rate of inflation and the level of unemployment.

The Federal Reserve Bank is an independent government agency in the sense that its policies are not reviewable by Congress or the president. It is governed by a seven-member board of directors, appointed by the U.S. president and confirmed by the Senate for 14-year terms. The U.S. president also appoints the chairman of the board, with Senate confirmation, for a four-year term. Within the system, there are twelve regional Federal Reserve Banks and an additional twenty-four branch banks. Each of the twelve regions has a board that is appointed by the national board and member banks.

Until 1980, the FED had broad regulatory powers over all the nation's banks. This included strict rules about what each sort of financial institution could and could not do with its money. But between 1980 and 1989 Congress approved a significant amount of deregulation. This was in keeping with the establishment of the New World Order. At the time many people argued that this would give financial institutions the leeway to "be competitive" in modern financial markets. Yet in the aftermath a number of banks failed due to highly speculative and unwise lending and investment activities. Hardest hit were savings and loan associations, which took full advantage of deregulation during Democrat Jimmy Carter's administration, and made all sorts of unwise investments with depositors' money. In 1982, S&L's lost their shirts to the tune of $200 billion dollars. Since the deposits were insured, the government had to pay up and most of the so-called "thrifts" went under, never to return.

Despite being relatively independent of the Federal Government, The FED has throughout its history been supportive and influential in developing dominant economic policies of both presidents and Congresses The three men who have successively chaired the FED since 1979—Paul Volker, Alan Greenspan, Ben Bernanke—have all contributed to policies supportive of turning debt into a commodity which propped up consumer spending even as living wage jobs were destroyed and incomes for many stagnated. They have also been supportive of monetary policies that contributed to relocating manufacturing, service employment and capital outside the U.S.

Paul Volker was the FED chair from 1979-87. His public image is that of a maverick who defied the stereotype of the Wall Street Operative. Yet he played a critical role in the birth of New World Order policies. Early in his career, he worked for the New York Federal Reserve and for Chase Manhattan Bank. He was an active member of the "Trilateral Commission," an organization spearheaded by Chase Manhattan Bank's David Rockefeller, which promoted policies to lower labor's share of value. And, as we have seen, these policies were at the heart of eventual New World Order restructuring after the end of the Bretton Woods era.

In the early 1970s, Volker was a key staff member of the U.S. Department of Treasury. He played an important role when President Nixon suspended the dollar-gold conversion in 1973, effectively cancelling the Bretton Woods Agreement. He was appointed to be the chair of the Federal Reserve by President Carter and reappointed by Ronald Reagan. During his tenure at the FED his policies were credited with ending "stagflation" (simultaneous unemployment and inflation) which was a major manifestation of a *crisis of value*. He did this through the FED, by pushing interest rates above 20%. This brought down the rate of inflation, a policy favored by the finance sector. But high interest rates also contributed to a high level of unemployment as well as inflating the exchange rate of the dollar. This made U.S. exports expensive and contributed to inflation, higher debt costs and economic decline in many developing nations. And this, in turn, opened these nations to economic penetration by both U.S. industry and finance.

Alan Greenspan, who was appointed by President Ronald Reagan and reappointed by Presidents George H.W. Bush, William Clinton, and George W. Bush, succeeded Volker. He has been strongly associated with the philosophy of novelist and philosopher Ayn Rand who espoused individual pursuit of happiness through free market capitalism with minimal to zero government interference. Greenspan was fully on board with the de-regulation of banks, much of which occurred during his tenure. He was also more outspoken about policies being debated by Congress, including the importance of tax cuts and the privatization of Social Security, particularly favored by the finance sector. Prior to his appointment to the FED, he coordinated the domestic policy positions of the Nixon campaign and later served as President Ford's chief economic advisor. After his tenure as FED chair, he formed a private consulting firm that advised many investment firms and large banks. He has served on the Board of Directors of at least eight corporations, including J.P. Morgan.

In 2008, in the heat of the financial meltdown, he was hired as an advisor to Paulson & Company, the fourth largest hedge fund in the world. At the time, Paulson was making a fortune by betting against a number of large banks and financial institutions that were heavily invested in subprime mortgages. It is not known what advice Greenspan gave, but during his tenure as FED chairman, he had "overlooked" the housing bubble; its rapid deflation gave rise to the crisis of 2007-8 and continues to this day. He had also turned a blind eye to the purchase of securities by Wall Street, including sub-prime mortgages. In any case, Paulson & Company, which had a large stake in Bank of America, opposed proposals to negotiate with mortgage holders facing foreclosure. Their successful opposition to negotiation protected Paulson's bets against subprime derivatives. And they made a fortune on these bets.

President Bush appointed the current FED chairman, Ben Bernanke, in 2006. Bernanke, a former economics professor at Princeton University, has been associated with the Federal Reserve System and government economic policy for more than a decade. In 2002, President Bush appointed him to a 14-year term on the FED Board of Governors. In 2005, Bush tapped him to be his Chief Economic advisor; he served in that capacity for one year. Bush then appointed him to another 14-year term with the FED, with a four-year term as chairman. President Obama reappointed him as chairman in 2010. As FED chairman he has played a major role in developing and exercising government policies to bail out the banks since the 2007 crash.

Bernacke oversaw the Troubled Assets Relief (TARP) program that pumped money into banks that were failing due to speculation on mortgage-backed securities. Along with pumping additional money into the banks, he orchestrated the bailout of the American Insurance Group (AIG), which got in trouble for selling

David Ranney

"credit default swaps," the insurance policies that guaranteed mortgage-backed securities and collateralized debt obligations. He is a firm believer in finance-friendly economic theories, which contend that nothing can go wrong in the economy that can't be solved by increasing the supply of money. Under Bernanke, the FED has made liberal use of what they call "quantitative easing"—buying government bonds in the open market—which pumps more money into the economy. He famously stated that, "The U.S. government has a technology called the printing press (or today, its electronic equivalent) that allows it to produce as many dollars as it wishes at no cost." His policies of increasing money supply have been controversial, but President Obama vigorously came to his defense during his reappointment hearings. As I write, Bernanke has announced that he will step down when his term ends. I predict his successor will continue the approach of his predecessors.

The Federal Reserve Bank has thus consistently been a key player in promoting and implementing economic policies that bolster government's mission to maintain a global and national capitalist system in which the U.S. remains the "most powerful nation in the world," where purchasing power depends on debt being a tradable commodity, and where profit rates depend on producing value without adequately compensating the producers. This mission explains the shifts I have traced in government efforts to provide social and merit needs, in the growth of inequality, and in stabilization polices in which the FED plays a leading role. The mission explains the current confusion around the "fiscal cliff" and it explains why, as the current crisis of value deepens, the FED continues to be governed by representatives of the finance sector, and supports banking policies and practices that played a major role in the initial collapse. These contradictory actions are a part of the churning and flailing that always accompany a *crisis of value*.

5. Churning and flailing is, in fact, the best way to describe all of government economic policy today. As the *crisis of value* deepens, there is genuine confusion about what to do. The confusion has the look and feel of political contentiousness. Yet there is a remarkable range of political agreement. No one (in politics or among policy wonks) has considered ditching the New World Order system. Most everyone seems to be against deficit spending and agree that there is no time like the present to bring down the size of the public debt. Interest rates are as low as they can go. Presidents Bush and Obama both proposed bailing out banks and increasing government spending as a "stimulus package." And the "fiscal cliff" and "sequester" debates contain contradictory elements; tax cuts to stimulate the economy and spending cuts that will do just the opposite. *The mark of churning and flailing is the unity we have around failed and failing policies.* The faltering of the U.S. system has not been lost on other parts of the world. The global policies and programs that enable physical and financial capital to be mobile have been termed the "Washington Consensus." Yet these are being resisted in some parts of the world, sometimes with physical force. At a time when U.S. government expenditures are being cut, military needs are growing.

d. U.S. Militarism

In the 2012 Federal budget, security spending, including Defense Department and Homeland Security, constituted 63% of the discretionary budget (spending not mandated by law but decided each year by Congress). The wars in Afghanistan and Iraq alone cost an estimated $159 billion in 2012, which was 12% of discretionary spending. In the past four years, President Obama has greatly increased drone attacks in Pakistan and other parts of the world. He has also endorsed a program under The National Defense Authorization Act of 2011 to arrest, imprison and detain indefinitely without trial persons suspected of involvement with terrorism. The U.S. aided the opposition to the regime in Libya, has threatened both Iran and North Korea over their nuclear programs, and briefly invaded Pakistan to assassinate Osama bin Laden. Domestic and foreign spying activities have increased to offset threats, real and imagined, of terrorism. The extent of that activity came to light when Edward Snowden, an intelligence analyst for the secretive National Security Agency (NSA), revealed a massive domestic surveillance program that includes domestic phone calls and Internet use. The U.S. maintains its special prison in Cuba for terrorism suspects. As I write, President Obama has also given official recognition to the opposition in Syria, and has sent missiles and troops to Turkey. He has also threatened to launch a military strike against Syria in retaliation for their use of chemical weapons during their civil war.

The U.S. has also militarized its borders, especially the border with Mexico. A recent opinion piece in the *New York Times* described the U.S.-Mexican border as a "war zone" full of defense contractors, sophisticated military technology and weapons, including Predator B drones. (Todd Miller, "War on the Border," *The New York Times* August 18, 2013. Miller's article is based on his recent book, (2014) *Border Patrol Nation: Dispatches From the Front Lines of Homeland Security*. San Francisco, CA: City Lights Open Media.) Miller described the Border Patrol as the nation's largest law-enforcement agency. Its mission is described as an "uneasy mixture" of counterterrorism, immigration and drug enforcement. Since September 11, 2001, the Border Patrol has spent $90 billion in border enforcement. Since 1993, the number of agents has increased from 4,000 to 16,000, and a pending "immigration reform" would increase that ten-fold. In 2012, it was estimated that border enforcement spending was $18 billion, which is 24% more than the budgets of the F.B.I., the Secret Service, the Drug Enforcement Agency, the Marshals Service and the Bureau of Alcohol, Tobacco, Firearms, and Explosives combined.

Despite the fiscal crisis, including budget deficits and a growing national debt, military expenditures continue to dominate federal spending. President Obama recently announced that he is reducing the size of the military but will rely on drones and special operations forces to carry on wars in the future. Despite its remarkable similarity to the Bush era programs under Secretary of Defense Donald Rumsfeld, Obama's plan has been greeted with howls of protest from Republicans (with the exception of Ron Paul) who complain that this will make the U.S. weak. Republican Presidential candidate Ron Paul proposed in a Republican presidential primary debate that we apply the "golden rule" to relations among nations—treat all nations the way we would like to be treated by them. The largely right-wing Christian audience loudly booed him, the other candidates derided him and the media dismissed him. This comes from some of government's greatest "deficit hawks" who have generally argued that deficit spending will mean U.S. ruin. Even President Obama's proposed cuts still place security related spending at a level that dwarfs every other budget category.

These hypocrisies and the decade of wars in the Middle East cause one to wonder why the U.S. Government, representing the interests of global corporations (many based in the U.S.), continues to exhaust the nation, the treasury and even the capacity of the military itself. And why the boos and derision directed at Ron Paul? Despite claims to the contrary, President Obama's policies promise to continue the broader program of perpetual war that prevailed before he took office. Only now he wants the job done by drone bombings and special operations strikes. Perpetual war appears to be in the political mainstream; it has achieved the status of common sense.

There is undoubtedly widespread fear in the U.S. body politic that any number of nations or terrorist groups could launch a 9-11 style attack. And politicians play to these fears, whipping up hysteria. The Obama administration has participated in the fear mongering as well, as he flexes his muscles in triumph over the high tech/special ops murder of Osama bin Laden and continues to bomb villages in the Pashtunistan region of Pakistan, Afghanistan and in the nation of Yemen.

But the question remains: Why address the post-9-11 fears of U.S. citizens with military aggression in the first place? Why are politicians of both parties trying so hard to look tough, and "stand tall" while killing civilians as well as militants, assassinating actual or suspected terrorist leaders, saber-rattling with Iran and North Korea, turning the U.S. borders into a war zone, spying on people everywhere (including inside the U.S.) while deepening the present *crisis of value*?

A few things are clear. There are very real threats against the U.S. The world is riddled with instability practically everywhere.

The global economic crisis has brought with it a global political crisis. And as long as the U.S. believes it needs to maintain its position in the world order as "the most powerful nation in the world" it must use military force to deal with disorder and threats against the U.S. and the entire global capitalist system. But again there is a contradiction here. *The U.S. must use military power to maintain the New World Order system. At the same time, the use of that power actually deepens the economic crisis and mobilizes many peoples around the world to attack the U.S.*

1. The Evolution of a Contradiction

The evolution of this contradiction, and the present militaristic churning and flailing go back to the evolution of the New World Order system itself. The New World Order promoted inequality between nations and within nations, leading to instabilities. Some nations began to resist being a part of the global regime because it required opening up their economies and their cultures to penetration and control by the emerging global corporations, a distinct loss of sovereignty. The U.S. government exercised its global dominance through the rules of the World Trade Organization and other "trade agreements"—like the North American Free Trade Agreement (NAFTA)—and through its control over the policies of the World Bank and the International Monetary Fund. Nations with their own resources, such as those in the Middle East and parts of South America, attempted to opt out of the New World Order rules, creating what the U.S. Department of Defense called a "globalization gap."

The gap included areas of the world that global capital could not control economically. Also, within many poorer nations that had been penetrated by the new regime, inequality grew as the influx of capital and industry combined with privatizations enriched the few at the expense of much of the population. A rise in food prices in nations like Tunisia and Egypt where up to half of people's income went to food has, as I noted earlier, been associated with the trading of commodity index funds. These price increases contributed to massive revolt. And growing wealth and income inequality contributed to both internal political instability as well as the rise of individual and organized crime.

I have already explained why the New World Order instituted in the 1980s was not sustainable; there was no real value behind the extension of loans and the trading of debt. Treating debt as a commodity and passing it around the globe and into the coffers of banks, hedge funds, retirement accounts and investment portfolios softened this contradiction. But it was truly a massive Ponzi scam. The saga of Bernie Madoff was just a microcosm of the larger system, but like Bernie's scam the global system could not continue. The bursting of the housing bubble initiated the collapse of this house of cards while rising food prices resulted in hunger and even starvation in many places in the world.

2. Militarism and the New World Order

Even before the housing bubble collapse in 2008 exposed the contradictions of a regime built on fictitious capital, phantom markets and phantom products, instabilities within and among nations began to appear. Built into the system was a dominant role for both the U.S. government and its corporations, which included a leading role in protecting the system when threatened by the instabilities it generated. The attack on September 11, 2001, was a dramatic reminder of both the dangers inherent in the world order and the responsibility of the U.S. to protect not just its citizens but also the system itself.

Even before the 9/11 attack, the Pentagon had articulated in some detail the actual and potential security threats to the global system, as well as a military strategy to deal with it. During the Secretary Rumsfeld period under President George W. Bush (2001-2006), the Office of Defense Transformation generated a world map on which were plotted U. S. Military responses to "situations" between 1990 and 2002. The map demonstrated that nearly all of these responses had been in parts of the world termed "the globalization gap." They concluded, "If you are fighting against or losing to globalization, you are likely a problem for the U.S." (Department of Defense, Office of Defense Transformation PowerPoint presentation during Donald Rumsfeld's tenure as Secretary of Defense. See: Arthur Cebrowski (2003, June 12). Planning a Revolution: Mapping the Pentagon's Transformation. *Heritage Foundation WebMemo* #292. www.heritage.org. Also, Thomas P.M. Barnett (2004). *The Pentagon's New Map*. New York, NY: Putnam.)

This outlook spawned a new defense strategy. The Pentagon argued that in this era of "globalization" there was a need to go beyond the old concept of "security equals defense." Pentagon planners introduced the term "transactions strategy" that involved *anticipating* security problems, then taking action to prevent them from occurring. The strategy attempted to integrate the global economic policy of the Treasury and Commerce Departments, foreign policy of the State Department, energy policy and security.

Pentagon planners articulated specific implications for security strategy that included a policy of preventive war, greater emphasis on special operations forces, a major emphasis on high tech surveillance and intelligence gathering, and a focus on eradicating "weapons of mass destruction." They also articulated the sort of weapons required, including the use of drones.

Overall, Pentagon planners envisioned a military strategy in which elite forces could use preemptive strikes that would cripple their targets with overwhelming force ("shock and awe") in a very short period of time. The military could strike in many places within the globalization gap zone on short notice whenever trouble loomed. These ideas initially appeared as public policy in the National Security Strategy document of September 2002. They were elaborated on in the National Security Strategy document of 2006 and the Quadrennial Defense Review of 2006. (Key staff person Thomas P.M. Barnett helped to develop these strategies and has since become a private consultant to the military. He has written a number of books expanding on these ideas.)

These policies were initially implemented in Iraq and Afghanistan. The 9/11 attacks and the rise of a stateless terror network were the first major tests for the U.S. military role in subduing non-compliant forces in the globalization gap. The policies in practice greatly underestimated the strength of an insurgency and proved to be a monumental failure. Suddenly the U.S. was bogged down in a long war rather than a quick hit, in and out affair prescribed by the National Security Strategy Document. As other problems surfaced in the globalization gap, the U.S. and its NATO allies found themselves stretched too thin. The long war was exacerbating the economic problems embedded in the New World Order system they were supposed to protect.

When the Obama Administration took office it was widely recognized that Iraq and Afghanistan constituted a quagmire for the U.S. and the entire New World Order system. President Obama decided the U.S. should begin to pull out of Iraq, but wanted to use the troops that were released to expand operations in Afghanistan. Bob Woodward's book, *Obama's Wars*, and President Obama's *National Security Strategy* document suggest that the analysis and strategy initially developed by the Bush Administration, and built on the logic of the globalization gap, was still the basis for military planning and security strategy. Now the question became one of how to implement the strategy as the economy collapsed, and how to apply the strategy successfully once it had failed in Iraq.

Inside the White House, the debate was between those who favored military action—focused mainly on destroying stateless terror groups like Al Qaeda—versus those who favored building new societies that would become part of the core of global capitalism. These two strategies came to be known as *counterterrorism* vs. *counterinsurgency*. Woodward's *Obama's Wars* suggests that since there were strong advocates of both approaches, Obama accepted a sort of hybrid of the two that had been pushed by Vice President Biden. Therefore, the accepted U.S. role of enforcer against opposition to the New World Order of global capital continued.

While the rhetoric of preventive war was dropped, the idea of military action aimed at groups and nations in the "globalization gap" remained in place. Likewise, eliminating weapons of mass destruction in the globalization gap remains. Use of drones and Special Forces to go after "terrorists" (counterterrorism) has now been combined with the use of military (both U.S. regular forces and Afghan police and soldiers) to protect civilians and secure cities and villages (counterinsurgency).

Since the acceptance of a hybrid strategy between counterterrorism and counterinsurgency, the U.S. military and the Obama Administration have faced a number of events and challenges that have further shaped military planning and operations:

- The raid and assassination of Osama bin Laden seems to have increased the emphasis on counterterrorism. This CIA-led special operations attack has been increasingly followed by drone strikes in Pakistan and Yemen as well as Afghanistan.

- Mark Mazzetti's book, *Way of the Knife*, and Jeremy Scahill's *Dirty Wars* both detail the growing influence of the Central Intelligence Agency, that has been running special operations in a series of secret wars in Africa, Asia and the Middle East.

- President Obama has greatly increased the frequency of drone missile strikes in these areas. Between 2004 and 2007 there were 13 attacks in Pakistan, Somalia and Yemen. In 2008, there were 30. In 2009, the number rose to 54, and in 2010 it was 122. (Peter Gelling, October 10, 2011. Drone Wars, *Global Post*.)

- The so-called Arab Spring that has resulted in regime changes in Tunisia, Libya, Egypt, and a massive civil war in Syria, threaten to redefine the geography of the "globalization gap." As I write this, there continues to be a high level of uncertainty concerning the evolving nature of the regimes. There is similar uncertainty in both Iraq and

Afghanistan as an insurgency continues. The attack on the U.S. consulate in Libya during which the U.S. Ambassador was killed brought this uncertainty into bold relief. Libya was a nation where the U.S. attempted to implement the hybrid military strategy by contributing to the elimination of the Muammar Gaddafi regime, while helping to build a new regime that could become a part of the New World Order system. In Egypt, the U.S. lost an important ally when the dictator, Hosni Mubarak, was overthrown. The nature of the new Egyptian regime is presently being contested.

• The outcome of the brutal civil war in Syria challenging the dictator Bashar al Assad is another element of Middle East uncertainty. Assad, and his father before him have ruled in Syria since 1971. The nation has been considered by both U.S. Republican and Democratic administrations to be a part of the "globalization gap." The Bush Administration considered Syria an enemy of the U.S. The brutality of the regime and its stance against U.S. dominance of the New World Order meant that the U.S. sided with the rebels. Assad's opposition, however, is a mixture of Sunni Islamists who reject New World Order policies and the U.S.'s global role, and more "moderate" forces that are presently more accepting of U.S. dominated programs. For this reason there are divisions in the U.S. and in Europe over whether to arm the rebels. President Obama has sent arms to Turkey, a strong U.S. ally, who is on Syria's border and is receiving Syrian refugees and opposition leaders.

- The Syrian war is also spilling into Lebanon, as Lebanese Shiite Muslim fighters associated with the political faction Hezbollah (considered by the U.S. to be a terrorist organization) have begun fighting on the side of the Assad regime as well as supplying it with arms. Iran backs Hezbollah. Israel and most Arab Sunni-dominated states fear the growing power of Iran—they want to see Assad's regime in Syria gone. Russia is aligned with Assad and vetoes any unfriendly resolutions or actions in the United Nations Security Council. Much of this came to a head when President Obama announced the U.S. would retaliate against the Assad regime after their brutal chemical attack killed civilians and children. U.S. citizens, tired of perpetual war, immediately responded negatively, as did Russia and China, who refused to sanction such an attack. In the end Syria agreed to destroy their stock of chemical weapons under United Nations supervision. But the civil war continues, and as it widens and spreads to other nations, there is great confusion in U.S. policy circles and the Obama Administration over what should be done.

- The turmoil in this region of the world has had an impact on the U.S. relationship to Israel. This nation has been a U.S. ally and the recipient of U.S. economic and military aid for many years. In 1948, the U.S. was the first to recognize Israel as a nation and has given Israel aid ever since. The U.S. was initially motivated by the U.S./Soviet Union Cold War conflict. The U.S. felt it needed to establish a solid base of support in the region. But even though the Cold War ended, support for the Israeli state has increased; it is now a vital part of the New World

Order system in the region. Beginning in 1976, the U.S. increased its military and economic aid to Israel. Since 1985, U.S. aid has amounted to roughly $3 billion a year. Palestine, which has contested Israeli occupation, is considered to be part of the "globalization gap." There are real questions about the status of other nations in the area like Egypt, Iraq, and Syria. Iran is decidedly in the globalization gap. And conflict, potentially very violent, over Iran's nuclear program threatens.

- In the build up of tensions around Iran's nuclear program, the crash of a U.S. drone in Iran demonstrated that the U.S. was using this technology for surveillance in Iranian airspace. This could be viewed as more of a counterterrorism operation.

- While the U.S. has withdrawn most U.S. troops from Iraq, they did so in part because the Iraqi Government, a product of U.S. counter-insurgency operations, refused terms demanded by the Obama Administration that would have allowed more of them to stay.

- Recently, there has been an uptick in attacks on Sunni politicians and citizens in Iraq. It has been charged that the Shiite led government is at least complicit in the violence.

- The role of the U.S. in Libya, with much heavier involvement by NATO forces, suggests that the U.S. plans to continue its role as enforcer in the Middle East though without "boots on the ground." That was likely necessitated by its continued heavy presence in both Iraq and Afghanistan.

- The expansion of bombings and drone strikes into Pakistan and the raid on the compound where Osama bin Laden was hiding have contributed to a rift between the military and civilian government in that country. The Pakistani military seems determined to push the U.S. out of the country. The new Prime Minister, Nawaz Sharif, has taken a strong position against U.S. use of drones in his country, yet he has expressed a desire to cooperate with the U.S. President Obama seems to be pulling back a bit from the use of drone strikes for fear of losing Pakistan to anti- U.S. Islamists.

The announcement by President Obama and former Secretary of Defense Leon Panetta that the military will shrink its forces and emphasize high-tech weaponry and special operations forces appears to swing back in the direction of Rumsfeld-era military planning. It likely represents a continued determination to play a key role as enforcer within the "globalization gap" despite the reality of a depleted military in the midst of a huge global economic crisis.

There is one more development of U.S. militarism that falls outside of the purview of the traditional military or the intelligence services. I refer to the huge build up of military operations on the U.S. borders discussed earlier. The movement of economic activity around the world that is central to the New World Order system has included massive displacement of people, including both war-related and economic migrations. Some of this movement of people has included the U.S., long a destination for immigrants around the world. This continues to be the case, but has intensified since the New World Order programs have been put in place. The U.S.-Canada-Mexico agreement known as the North American Free Trade Agreement (NAFTA) promised greater economic opportunities for Mexicans. But in reality, the movement of industry both in and out of Mexico has caused massive dislocation of Mexicans and other nationals south of the U.S. border. NAFTA initially contributed to rural dislocation in Mexico as farm populations were forced out of rural areas and into so-called *maquiladora* districts, which employ workers in foreign-owned factories. These manufacturing activities displaced other Mexican businesses and their employees. Eventually many of the *maquiladora* factories moved out of Mexico to countries like China and Korea. These dislocations created more pressure to find jobs in the U.S. and also contributed to the growth of the drug cartels.

Each year about one million people are granted legal immigration status in the U.S. (Randall Monger & James Yankay. *U.S. Legal Permanent Residents: 2012, March 2013, U.S. Homeland Security Annual Flow Report*) But large numbers of people cross the borders without U.S. government permission. The Pew Research Center has estimated that there are 11 million undocumented workers in the U.S. (Brian Resnick, May 30, 2013: *National Journal*). 63% have lived in the U.S. for more than ten years. Immigrant rights organizations have for a long time challenged U.S. laws and the violations of immigrant rights. Since 9/11, when the U.S. Government and many of its citizens heightened efforts to seal the borders and root out "illegals," immigrant rights protests and demands for immigration law reform have been on the rise. So has anti-immigrant activity. This political dynamic has been heightened as the *crisis of value* deepens due to greater competition for jobs. On one hand, the result has been a huge anti-immigrant backlash, heightened by the declared "war on drugs" and post 9/11 fears of "outsiders." On the other are legislative proposals to reform immigration law. The net effect has been the militarization of the border, and current immigration legal reform proposals stipulate that the borders become militarized even more.

3. Why the U.S. Government and Military Do What They Do

This gets us back to the question I began with. In what sense are the military, intelligence and border activities outlined above helping to protect the New World Order system? And specifically what does the U.S. government, which is charged with protecting the system, get out of such costly, contentious and unpopular activities? To answer this we need to review how the current situation evolved. Clearly, after World War II, the U.S. government and its large industrialists benefited greatly from being the center of global capitalism. The rebuilding of Europe and Japan using U.S. products and firms brought wealth into the U.S. It also enabled U.S capital to pacify its own working classes by paying higher wages and offering a "middle class" lifestyle— houses, cars, education—to the white working class in the suburbs.

The main threat to this state of affairs came from the Soviet Union and to a lesser extent China. From the perspective of a world capitalism dominated by U.S. corporations, the formation of NATO with the U.S. at the helm, policing the world, was rational. As this regime came to an end in the late 1960's, the new regime that included high economic integration, and capital mobility fueled by fictitious capital in the form of debt commodities, also had to be protected. With global economic integration, there was now a more international flavor to the elites who had the most to gain (or lose) in the maintenance of the new regime. The Euro-zone nations, most old NATO allies, Israel, and even Russia and China now contained blocks of capital fully vested in the New World Order system of mobile capital and debt trading. The boards of directors of the world's largest banks came from all over the world. Their assets included derivatives whose underlying assets were also from all over the world. And they all seemed to agree that the U.S. military needed to take the lead in defending this global empire.

Conditions have changed since the system began to take shape in the mid 1980s. They have changed since the roaring 1990s when speculation was making a lot of people around the world very wealthy. What is changing is that the contradictions in this regime have heightened to the point of global crisis. Not unlike previous shifts in the nature of the global capitalist system, there is a high degree of uncertainty about the future direction of global capital. There are new players who are ready to take advantage of the situation by taking global capitalism in a new direction, or trying to destroy it. As at similar junctures in history there is presently a great deal of churning and flailing. So part of the answer to the question of why the U.S. is doing what it is doing in the Middle East is that much of world capitalism expects it to maintain the lead in policing the globalization gap. Who else would do it? Who could do it better? At stake is not just a U.S. Empire but a global regime.

This begs the question of U.S. involvement in Iraq and particularly Afghanistan. It is difficult to make an objective case that these nations are a threat to the global regime. The spread of Al Qaeda-like organizations may be a threat. But Afghanistan, even in the hands of the Taliban is not. This, however, was also the case in Vietnam. The argument for that war was the domino effect of a Communist Vietnam. After the U.S. lost the war, not only did the dominos fail to fall, the Soviet system itself fell and China took the capitalist road. The answer, I believe, is that we remain in both Iraq and Afghanistan because we don't know how to get out without highlighting the vulnerability and weakness of the U.S. led global regime.

Our New World Order *is* vulnerable, weak, and in the midst of a deep structural economic crisis. And there are rivals to U.S. power waiting in the wings, which may well challenge the U.S. and even Euro zone nations for control of the system. The BRICS nations—Brazil, Russia, India, China and South Africa—are just some of a number of possibilities. Decision makers in the U.S. as well as those blocs of capital around the world vested in the present New World Order system, still depend on the U.S. military to continue to protect the regime. For those who believe in the globalization gap thesis, losing to the Taliban in Afghanistan might well be perceived as a profound weakness in the entire system. The rationale used by the players in the present global regime for the U.S. to fight these wars is less economic than it is political and subjective.

e. Government, Politics and the New World (Dis)order

The strategy of global elites to reduce labor's share of global value, which was crafted in the 1970s and implemented throughout the 1980s and 1990s, can be judged a "success." This strategy involved the rise of a new "common sense" that incorporated ideas and associated programs that had been in development since the 1940s—neoliberalism on the economic front and neoconservatism in social policies. Ironically, the

153

measures of its "success" included the growing inequality and political instability in the U.S., the increasingly impoverished working classes of Europe, and the sweatshops of Asia, Africa and Latin America where value was created by peoples living in abject poverty. The implementation of this New World Order, as I have shown, included the destruction of claims on value by eliminating higher wage jobs and shipping them in bits and pieces around the world. So-called trade agreements, and the structural adjustment programs of the IMF and World Bank drove many peasants from the land and into their nations' sweatshops. Global capital, and the governments that represented global capital now controlled the economies of many developing nations. And, as the contradictions of the New World Order began to appear in the millennium years, harsh austerity measures were imposed on the nations of Europe and the United States.

In the U.S., the shift in common sense, the nature of American elections, the evolving economic and social policies and militarism are all geared to protect, and not to challenge, the New World Order. Since its inception the contradictions embedded in this order have appeared as a global crisis of value. A government and politics that are designed to keep the system intact contribute to its self-destruction. It is now a system that attempts to resolve the contradiction in which there are more claims on value than the system is capable of producing. This is done through the development and protection of phantom markets, phantom products and fictitious capital. Spending, taxing and printing money can't fix a system built on such a foundation. Neither neoliberalism nor neo-Keynesianism address this contradiction. And it can't be fixed by using the stick of militarism to put down the revolts that are now emerging worldwide.

David Ranney

The *crisis of value* that we are experiencing today can possibly be fixed through another brutal round of destruction of claims on value and a thorough reorganization of the system, as occurred both in the 1940s and again in the 1980s. Or, the contradiction can be resolved by a revolution in thought and a totally new system that abolishes value based on labor. The latter could go in a number of directions and not all of them would be good for humanity. *But presently the New World Order is better described as the new world disorder.*

Discussion Questions

1. Explain the author's conception of phantom markets?
2. The author contends "global capitalism today has reached a point where the very features that in theory make markets efficient are disappearing." What does he mean by that?
3. In what sense does the normal functioning of markets in the "New World Order" contribute to its destruction?
4. What, according to the author, is the fundamental purpose of government? Do you agree?
5. What is the meaning and significance of the concept of "common sense"?
6. What is the function of the U.S. Federal Reserve Bank?
7. How does U.S. military policy relate to the "New World Order"?
8. How does the present *crisis of value* impact U.S. militarism?

Chapter 5
Some Prospects

"I don't know how that's goin' to end."

Thornton Wilder, *Our Town*

From time to time I give public lectures or conduct workshops covering some of the topics included in this book. Invariably, I get asked three questions: 1) So, what should I do with my retirement savings? 2) What is going to happen in the future? 3) What would you do if you were in charge? To the first question, I suggest they convert their savings to gold and bury it in the forest. (Be sure to make an accurate map.) To the second, I say I have no idea—when I studied economics, my professor advised against making forecasts. But if you do, he said, make the future so long range that you'll be dead or at least retired before the validity of your predictions can be invalidated.

In this concluding chapter I will address questions 2 and 3. As to the future, rather than make predictions, I will offer a range of scenarios or possibilities along with my assessment of many of them. Which of these, if any, become reality is largely up to all of us. We can get together to oppose some possibilities and advocate for others. In this spirit, I will also offer my view of the sort of world I would like for the future.

This book has argued that capitalism has a tendency toward periodic crisis that I have termed a *crisis of value*. This is a crisis where the claims on the value that the system as a whole produces, become greater than the amount of value the system is capable of producing. Since the beginnings of capitalism in the early 1800's, there have been crises of value. In each case, the system responded with a period of what I have called *churning and flailing* during which claims on value were destroyed and the system was restored on a new basis. The period between 1960 and 1980 was a time of churning and flailing involving war, accelerated environmental degradation and the collapse of manufacturing in the U.S. and other industrialized nations.

Churning and flailing is also a time of social upheaval. People rise up and oppose the system that is hampering their efforts to live a decent life. At times, such movements open up a glimpse of possibilities for a different kind of world. In the 1960-80 period we had a great civil rights movement in the U.S., an anti war movement and a period of labor insurgency. During this period an environmental movement was born. But none of these prevailed. Instead a new form of capitalism evolved.

In place of the prior system that depended on mass production in industrialized nations, the U.S. took the lead in establishing a "New World Order." The New World Order is a system in which 1) the U.S is "the most powerful nation in the world," 2) purchasing power depends on debt being a tradable commodity and, 3) profit rates depend on producing value without adequately compensating the producers. But at this time the historic capitalist crisis of value has reappeared. The New World Order has become a *new world disorder*. Below I will discuss four possible scenarios for the future in order to begin a discussion of "how this is goin' to end."

The first is that the U.S. and various allies will attempt to extend the present new world disorder by making it somewhat more orderly. I will argue that this will extend the period of churning and flailing with its attendant misery and chaos, and that it cannot resolve the present crisis of value.

Secondly, I will look at various challenges to U.S. domination of the system that are underway. The challenges to U.S. power I discuss here are those that seek to take over the new world disorder, leaving intact the system based on phantom markets, phantom products and fictitious capital. These options, like the U.S. effort to extend the present system, can drag on for some time but cannot ultimately resolve the crisis and ongoing disorder.

I will then discuss some of the efforts (by many of the same players) to try to restart capitalism on a new basis—a sort of *newer* New World Order. I will argue, however, that if these efforts prevail it will generate misery for much of the world's population, put the planet itself in greater peril, while keeping capitalism's historic tendency to generate crises of value firmly in place.

Finally, I'll consider prospects for an end to capitalism and its replacement by a new system altogether. While it is folly to assume that capitalism cannot persist in one form or another, it is equally false to assume that it can't be replaced by a truly new kind of society. I will examine two possibilities. One is the very real prospect of a new form of fascism.

And then, in opposition to fascism, I will conclude by describing a different kind of society, one that is both anti-fascist and a viable and revolutionary alternative to capitalism. *I will ask: what are the prospects of a society whose number one concern is the full and free development of all human beings.* Can we imagine a society where the measure of wealth is not money or "assets" but meeting human needs and enhancing human capacity and enjoyment? Can we consider the possibility that in such a society humans consider themselves to be a part of nature and their development is therefore in harmony with the natural environment?

1. More Churning and Flailing

It is quite likely that we are in for an extended period of churning and flailing. This is apt to be a very bumpy road that includes both economic and political instability as well as considerable violence. I begin a discussion of continuing elements of churning on a global scale and then focus on the U.S., as the government attempts to hang onto its leadership of the new world disorder.

a. Global "Intifada"

It has been particularly difficult to reflect on prospects for the future in the context of so many uprisings, coups, and wars around the world. One writer called this a "global intifada." Intifada is an Arabic word that literally means to "shake off" and is often translated into English as uprising. The word was first used by Palestinians to describe two uprisings against Israel in the years 1987-93 and again between 2000-2005. Since 2000, a global intifada has gone on unabated. In 2001, the suicide attack by Al Qaeda militants on the World Trade Center was answered initially by a U.S. attack on Afghanistan, followed by the invasion of Iraq in 2002. These attacks overthrew the regimes in both nations in short order. But once the Taliban was deposed in Afghanistan and Saddam Hussein was captured and executed in Iraq, the U.S. was faced with a fierce insurgency in both nations. This has resulted in more than a decade of war and a continued insurgency even as the U.S. pulls back its troops.

Then, in 2010 a period known as the "Arab Spring" resulted in the toppling of three dictatorial regimes in Tunisia, Libya and Egypt. The end of dictatorial regimes, however, has hardly resolved the crises. There remain serious opposition protests against the regimes in all of these North African countries. The most dramatic has been Egypt. In June and July of 2013, protests in Egypt dwarfed the earlier 2011 uprising that ended the reign of dictator Hosni Mubarak. They were the largest protests in that nation's history and prompted a military takeover that deposed Mubarak's elected successor, Muhammad Morsi.

Throughout the region there are both protests and war. Protests in 2012 against Syrian dictator Bashar al-Assad led to a military attack on the opposition and began a bloody and ruinous civil war. That war threatens to spill over into Lebanon. The regime in Turkey is facing serious protest-challenges. Protests during 2012-13 have also challenged the regimes in Bahrain, Yemen, Saudi Arabia, and Kuwait. And the conflict between Palestine and Israel that began with the two waves of intifada continues.

Protests and strikes are ongoing throughout Europe, Asia and Africa. The "indignados" protests in Spain and massive protests in Greece are a response to austerity measures imposed in areas where over a third of the people are unemployed and even more fail to earn enough to live on. Chinese factory workers contesting working conditions and low pay threaten China's economy, which depends on cheap exports. Workers in Bangladesh, the site of a horrific building collapse and factory fires, have begun worker rights campaigns as manufacturers attempt to cut costs to provide cheap clothes for New World Order players like Walmart. South African miners were massacred during a strike for livable wages and safer working conditions, and there are insurgencies against many other African regimes. Significant protests have also erupted in Brazil, whose leader, Dilma Rousseff, and her party, are generally seen as part of a progressive trend in South America. What started as a small protest against raising bus fares grew rapidly to include the government's decision to spend huge sums hosting international sporting events while so many of Brazil's citizens go hungry.

In the U.S., a wave of protests that initially challenged the financial heart of the New World Order was called "Occupy Wall Street." It then expanded to focus on the fact that the richest 1% of the U.S. is getting richer at the expense of practically everyone else. "We are the 99%" was the slogan of choice. This movement now seems to have run out of steam. And as we will see, the U.S. pushes on without addressing the contradictions within the new world *dis*order.

There are many other struggles that I haven't even mentioned, and the global intifada is still evolving. A look at the big picture reveals a number of things. Every place that the tentacles of The New World Order have reached has experienced the enrichment of the few at the expense of most. All of the struggles against regimes around the world begin with protests over how the ruling classes distribute the value created by global capitalism. These struggles only gain intensity as the global system's claims on value exceed what the system can generate. For those not in extreme poverty but who see their standards of living decline there are intensifying quality of life issues. The qualitative dimension of human development includes the distribution of benefits and costs of the present system. But there is also the decline of environmental quality, quality of education, health care and other public services, as well as human rights abuses, including the rights of indigenous peoples, women, and LGBT peoples. The quality of everyday life is an issue that affects all but the rich. The global intifada thus adds up to a massive response to the failing system. It is a part of the churning and flailing process that is raising questions about the viability of the system itself. Economists, policy experts and politicians who limit their solutions to only those that would make the New World Order more orderly do not begin to address the challenges most of us face. Such solutions would simply serve those who control and benefit from the present system. It really amounts to global and malignant neglect in the face of global intifada. This neglect has a number of aspects that pose as "public policy," addressed below.

b. Supply-Side vs. Demand-Side

There are no political or corporate leaders anywhere in the world calling for a rethinking of a system based on phantom markets, phantom products and fictitious capital. Nor is anyone calling for an end to dependency on the trading of debt as a commodity, or an end to a production system whose profit rates require unsustainable exploitation of those who produce value (even as global factories explode in Texas and implode in Bangladesh). Nor are there any U.S. based politicians who are willing to give up on the U.S. as the "most powerful nation in the world." They wish to hold onto this status even as the system sinks ever deeper into crisis. The political and economic leaders of the new world disorder are united in their desire to keep things pretty much as they are. What they disagree about is how to make the new world disorder slightly more orderly.

Most of the world's leadership is trying to bring down debt, but they are not trying to eliminate the reliance on debt that can be traded as a commodity. What is always proposed is some combination of tax cuts to stimulate the economy and spending cuts to do just the opposite! That logic is dominant in the European Union where austerity is being imposed on nations with unemployment rates ranging from 20% to nearly 30%. The contradictory nature of this strategy has led to riots and even threats of a new war in Europe. In the U.S., the Congress and the Obama Administration can't agree on a budget. As I write this, a ridiculous "compromise" is in force. "Sequestering" requires across the board cuts in all federal expenditures if Republican and Democrats can't agree on a budget that brings down the size of the national debt.

The unrest in Europe and the stalemate in Washington do not question the very system that created this mess. And politicians seem to agree that the problems, rather than being due to any contradiction in the system, can be fixed with greater economic growth. What they disagree about is what sort of economic policy can produce the most growth in terms of both production and jobs.

The Republican Party in the U.S. and conservative politicians in Europe tend to favor what economists call "supply-side" policies. They advocate low taxes and small government, which amounts to cutting services even as the crisis deepens. The theory behind this is that by cutting both taxes and government regulations and lowering debt, people who "can create jobs" will have more money with less government interference. They will then use it to invest in businesses that lead to jobs. The reality for many people, though, is austerity in a time when they have no jobs and therefore need more help from the government. (This is what the political confrontations in Greece and Spain are all about.) Supply-side policies were tried in the U.S. during The Reagan Administration, but new jobs created by those with more money and less government interference never appeared. This prompted the first President Bush to call it "voodoo economics."

Liberals in the U.S. who tend to be with the Democratic Party as well as those to the left of the Democratic Party and many in Europe, favor what economists call demand-side policies. In a period of economic crisis, they argue, government should spend money and also cut taxes, especially for those at the lower end of the economic spectrum. The idea is that this spending will stimulate economic growth, enabling us to grow our way out of the crisis. This political view is based roughly on the ideas of John Maynard Keynes, whom I have previously discussed. Even in places where demand-side policies have led to growth and reduced poverty, they have not begun to address the qualitative issues that include the distribution of income, the environment, health care, education and human rights. This is what the massive revolt in Brazil was all about. As the crisis deepens, both qualitative and quantitative deterioration will only deepen the resolve of the opposition.

In the U.S. these two poles have created a political stalemate— neither side can really put their ideas into practice. The liberals have accepted the idea that debt is too high but they want to increase taxes for the wealthy to pay for fewer cuts in social spending. The conservatives will have none of it, so at the time of this writing we are in a period called sequester. This idea, the worst of both worlds, suggests that as favorite programs from both sides are cut, compromise is possible. But what can a compromise really do about the crisis? President Obama's proposals have undermined the basis of demand-side ideas and even threaten programs that have little to do with the size of the debt, like Social Security and Medicare. The Republicans, for their part, allow small increases in taxes on the wealthy but insist on spending cuts that compromise the government's ability to address domestic needs at a time when unemployment is high and people are either living in misery or watching their living standards and quality of life decline.

Most importantly, neither supply-side nor demand-side policies address a crisis of value. If the heart of the matter is that the amount of value the system is capable of producing is not sufficient to meet the claims made on it, spending and taxing policies are at best irrelevant, and can even contribute to deepening the crisis. Taxes, as I have argued, are a claim on value. Increasing them can only increase the claims. And spending does not add value. Yet people still need government services and general support for health care and education. Even if some of these policies stimulate the growth of Gross Domestic Product, GDP does not measure the state of things in terms of the most fundamental issues of any economic system. As Paul Mattick in his very useful book, *Business as Usual,* puts it: "Profit is the money representation of the labor performed by employees of all of society's productive businesses in excess of the work required to replace raw materials, tools, and those employees themselves." Any economic system must be able to reproduce itself and the people who are part of it. If the system is not able to address this issue, neither supply-side nor demand-side or even a growing GDP can work. Today's stalemate in Washington is just so much churning and flailing of a system in crisis.

c. Permanent Fiscal Crisis

When state and local government spending and taxing are added to those generated by the Federal Government, public sector based claims on value are even greater. State government taxes are generally levied on income and the sales of the goods and services people need. Local governments tax real estate. All these taxes come out of personal incomes so they amount to additional claims on value. Shrinking government means that people will see a deterioration of schools, health care, highways and other infrastructure, police and fire protection, assistance buying food and many other vital needs. Expanding government means more unsustainable debt. When conservatives and liberals attack each other's economic policy ideas, they are essentially correct. As the crisis deepens so does the government fiscal crisis. As long as the effort to extend the life of the system continues, we will find ourselves in a state of "permanent" fiscal crisis.

d. Environmental Degradation

Earlier I argued that capitalism by its very nature tends to degrade the environment. But as degradation appears, public protest causes government—the protector of the system—to increase governmental regulation and incentives for the private sector to develop new technologies to help protect the earth. I also argued that the New World Order superseded such measures by increasing worldwide per capita consumption and by moving production to nations with fewer environmental protections. The entire point of the New World Order was to reduce claims on value by reducing production costs, including the costs of environmental cleanup.

There is an environmental dimension to the churning and flailing in the U.S. as the nation attempts to maintain control over global capitalism in a time of crisis. The consequences of a system of production that has created pollution and waste far beyond the earth's carrying capacity are becoming all too visible. The earth is warming, and with that has come severe weather patterns: frequent and devastating hurricanes, tornados, flooding and drought. The search for and exploitation of new energy sources and unregulated industrial development have polluted water supplies and greatly increased the amount of carbon dioxide in the atmosphere.

The amount of carbon dioxide (CO2) in the atmosphere impacts the temperature of the planet. CO_2 is a natural part of our air and absolutely necessary for survival as it keeps the planet warm enough for human survival. But energy consumption adds to the relative amount of carbon dioxide in the air (measured in parts per million, or ppm) to the extent that the planet is warming at an unprecedented rate. Many fear that further global warming could melt the Earth's ice caps, releasing methane gasses that would accelerate the warming of the planet. Most climate and earth scientists seem to agree that the maximum carbon dioxide composition of the air, without further warming effects, is 350 ppm. (350 ppm is a measure of the Earth's carrying capacity. Carrying capacity is the natural ability of the Earth's ecosystem to sustain itself.) Up until about 200 years ago the level had been stable at 275 ppm. It began to rise with the advent of industrialism and capitalism, due to increasing the use of fossil fuels for energy. We are now at 392 ppm and that number is growing at a rate of 2 ppm per year! (See www.350.org or environmentalist William McKibben's book, *Eaarth*.)

This state of affairs has gotten the attention of people and their political leaders around the world. As noted earlier, there have been international meetings and treaties, but these have had little impact on decision makers. In fact, some industrialists have launched counter campaigns against the science related above. They essentially contend that the warming of the planet is natural and more regulation or a decline in the consumption of energy will cause loss of jobs and increase poverty. As long as the new world disorder is maintained, they may be right! Reducing and stabilizing CO_2 ppm does involve increasing claims on value through regulation or decreasing production and hence value. So both sides of this conflict are part of the global churning and flailing that cannot be resolved without massive political, economic and social change.

e. Permanent War and a National Security State

Historically, as crises of value evolve, the period of churning and flailing that occurs includes global social upheaval. Today's global intifada, as I have argued, is such a response to the present crisis. Government, as the protector of the system it governs, steps in to try to contain or defeat the upheaval that accompanies crisis. And in this particular crisis, the U.S. Government has adapted its military mission and structure to confront nations and organizations that oppose the New World Order and U.S. control over the system. The U.S. Department of Defense has designated such nations as a "globalization gap." Organizations and nations that actively resist the global reach of the New World Order system are deemed "terrorist." Both military and intelligence activity in the U.S. assume the role of enforcer of New World Order policies and programs. But U.S. security strategy and activities constitute a contradiction. The enormous cost, both economic and human, contribute to the growing disorder and to the crisis itself. Yet, in order to maintain its status as the dominant force in the present global capitalist system, the U.S. is forced to pursue a militarism that combats those who threaten the system. This is the explanation for our heavy involvement in Iraq, Afghanistan, Pakistan, Yemen, Libya, and beyond. It also explains the growth of drone attacks. It explains the massive build-up of military forces on the U.S. borders. And it explains the revelations about the extent of spying on people living in the U.S. through monitoring Internet use, phone calls and e-mails. The U.S. is evolving into a national security state. It is, moreover, a nation in a perpetual state of war both within and outside its borders as the global crisis deepens and as individuals, groups and nations wage a global intifada against what has become the new world disorder.

Exactly how the evolution of the national security state will play out is impossible to predict. It is a work in progress. Its origins lie in the unraveling of the previous global system known as the Bretton Woods system. As the *crisis of value* for that system deepened, there was growing opposition to it around the world. From the very beginning, the leading force of opposition to the Bretton Woods system was the Soviet Union. That bloc contested U.S. domination of global capitalism primarily in its effort to gain access to the resources of the developing world. Similarly, U.S. military and intelligence policies and actions were primarily aimed at thwarting the Soviet's efforts to gain spheres of influence in the developing and resource rich nations. As the crisis of value deepened in the 1960s and 1970s there was a major anti-imperialist movement in these developing nations, which sought to put an end to the domination of Western powers. Within the U.S., militant civil rights and labor movements as well as the movement against the Vietnam War became increasingly anti-capitalist in tone and substance. These challenges shaped U.S. military and intelligence practices in the late 1960s and the early 70s.

The Vietnam War consumed the military, while the role of intelligence services—especially the Federal Bureau of Investigation (FBI) and Central Intelligence Agency (CIA)—evolved to meet both international and domestic challenges. Most domestic intelligence activity was done by the FBI in partnership with local and state police through a secret program known as the Counterintelligence Program or COINTELPRO. It was most active between 1956 and 1971. It included many covert programs that aimed to disrupt, destroy, demoralize, and discredit a wide array of labor, civil rights, socialist, antiwar and community organizations and the individuals who led or participated in them. Individuals were framed and put into prison. Some were assassinated.

The CIA also engaged in some domestic spying, most notably their infiltration of the National Student Association. But their main clandestine activities were directed at foreign governments, organizations and individuals who opposed the U.S. These activities included interfering with elections, aiding or directing coups against particular leaders, and assassination. In 1971 the existence of COINTELPRO became known, and protests came from a number of directions. Also, the involvement of the U.S. in assassination and covert actions abroad were revealed. Congress was accused of being too lax in their overview of intelligence activities and as a result, in 1975, the U.S. Senate formed a special committee to investigate. "The United States Senate Select Committee to Study Governmental Operations With Respect to Intelligence Activities" was chaired by Senator Frank Church. Ultimately they issued fourteen reports detailing what they considered were abuses of power by the FBI, CIA and the National Security Agency (NSA). In the aftermath of these reports a number of steps were taken to rein in the activities of the U.S. intelligence agencies. Three different executive orders by the Ford, Carter and Reagan Administrations banned U.S. sanctioned assassinations of foreign leaders and greatly curtailed spying on U.S. citizens. A variety of measures intended to monitor intelligence agencies were also put in place.

These measures did not completely halt abuses of intelligence activity but did subdue the agencies, especially the CIA. However, the current crisis of value and the challenges to U.S. power and the system in general have, in the last decade, brought about a major increase in both military and intelligence activities. There has been a great deal written about this subject. I found the analyses in Mark Mazzetti's *Way of the Knife* (2013, Penguin Press) and Jeremy Scahill's *Dirty Wars* (2013, Nation Books) especially useful. Mazzetti argues that the CIA has become increasingly powerful, especially under the Obama Administration. They have taken on combat operations that had traditionally been the domain of the Department of Defense in order to avoid Congressional oversight. And the CIA has actually neglected clandestine spy operations by either farming them out to private contractors or allowing the military to expand their intelligence activities.

In a number of operations, most notably the assassination of Osama bin Laden, the CIA had operational control over the Defense Department's Navy Seal Team 6 unit that actually conducted the raid. The CIA also runs the majority of armed drone strikes that target individuals for assassination. Scahill's book focuses more on how the CIA and special operations units of the military have been waging secret wars throughout the world by overcoming the bans on assassination that had been in force since the 1970s. I also drew insight from Bob Woodward's *Obama's Wars* that focuses on the strategy development of Obama's Defense Department and intelligence services in Iraq and Afghanistan just after Obama took office. Finally, I recommend Lawrence Wright's *The Looming Tower: al Qaeda and the Road to 9/11* (2006), which traces the history of the attack on the World Trade Center on September 11, 2001. It examines the history and formation of al Qaeda as well as the fumbles of both FBI and CIA in stopping the attack. Taken together these books paint a picture of an evolving U.S. national security state that is a part of the churning and flailing of a system in crisis, and of the U.S. effort to maintain its power in the world as the system crumbles.

The present *crisis of value,* and challenges both to the New World Order system and to U.S. power began to appear in the later years of the Clinton Administration. When George W. Bush came into office, his security advisors—especially Vice President Dick Cheney and Secretary of Defense Donald Rumsfeld—began to look for ways around the limits that had been placed on both the Department of Defense and the CIA. That effort was greatly enhanced by the attack on the World Trade Center on September

11, 2001. A combination of national legislation and executive orders swept away many of the protections and oversight provisions that had limited Defense Department and intelligence agency power in the wake of the Church Commission reports of the 1970s.

The Patriot Act was a key piece of legislation in this regard. Passed on October 26, 2001, this law greatly reduced restrictions on domestic spying where "terrorism" was concerned, and it expanded the definition of terrorism itself. It gave the intelligence services the ability to engage in "roving wiretaps" that included the Internet, searches of business records, cell phones and landlines. It made it easier to gain authorization for such activities by allowing government agencies to gather "foreign intelligence information" from persons within the U.S., citizen and non-citizen alike. It included targets considered to be "lone wolves," individuals not tied to any known terrorist groups. On May 26, 2011, President Obama signed an extension to continue Patriot Act authority.

Also, on September 14, 2001, the U.S. Congress passed a joint resolution known as the Authorization for the use Military Force (AUMF)] that was quickly signed by President Bush. The act essentially gave the President the right to wage war against "terrorists" all over the world. The AUMF states: "That the President is authorized to use all necessary and appropriate force against those nations, organizations, persons he determines planned, authorized, committed, or aided the terrorist attacks that occurred on September 11, 2001, or harbored such organizations or persons, in order to prevent any future acts of international terrorism against the United States by nations, organizations or persons." The AUMF remains in force today. It enabled the

President to attack both Afghanistan and Iraq as well as initiate drone strikes in Pakistan and Yemen. In his speech on May 23, 2013, President Obama noted that the AUMF was ten years old. He then stated his intention to get Congress to repeal the AUMF mandate and replace it with something else but indicated no timetable; nor did he specify what a new mandate might look like. While saying that his policies and drone strikes had diminished al Qaeda, Obama went on to emphasize a continuing threat from "al Qaeda and its associated forces from Yemen to Iraq, from Somalia to North Africa. He singled out "al Qaeda's affiliates in the Arabian Peninsula, AQAP" as well as "a real threat from radicalized individuals here in the United States." He justified the use of "lethal force" in the form of drone strikes as "effective" and "legal" and administered with "clear guidelines, oversight and accountability." Despite strong protests from Pakistan, particularly over the raid on Osama bin Laden's compound and a number of other strikes on the border of Afghanistan, he claimed, "our actions are bound by consultations with partners, and respect for state sovereignty." Two days after the speech there was another lethal strike on Pakistan.

In addition to AUMF, Congress also provides an annual military appropriation known as the National Defense Authorization Act (NDAA). It has become more than simply defense appropriations. In the 2012 and 2013, NDAA permitted the indefinite detention of both U.S. citizens and non-citizens who are considered to be "belligerents" and are seized overseas. The NDAA specified that they are not obligated to try such people in domestic courts but could use military tribunals, which do not have the same constitutional restrictions.

David Ranney

Another executive order by the Bush Administration that has helped shape the structure of the evolving national security state was issued September 17, 2001. It allowed security services to abduct individuals and hold them in "black sites" (secret prisons outside the U.S.) where they could be held indefinitely without charges. This practice is known as "extraordinary rendition." During the days of the Bush Administration this executive order allowed for a redefinition of torture, calling a variety of interrogation techniques such as waterboarding (simulating drowning by continuously pouring water over someone's face) "enhanced interrogation." President Obama put an end to the torture but instead encouraged the use of detention without charge, standard "legal" interrogation, and a shift away (on the part of the CIA) from snatching people for extraordinary renditions in favor of assassinating "high value targets."

These government actions provide a framework that is turning the U.S. into an evolving national security state that uses the dwindling resources of the nation to hold onto a U.S. dominated new world disorder. A number of aspects of the national security state have become commonplace; their existence and application is part of the common sense understanding of what government needs to do. People applauded military assault, including the total lockdown of the City of Boston as military swat teams quickly closed in on the two young men accused of placing bombs at the finish line of the Boston Marathon. In a display of the capabilities of a national security state, private homes were searched door to door and the population of a major American city was confined to their homes. It demonstrated that local, state and national military forces now have access to the latest in military equipment and logistical know-how to meet any sort of threat imaginable, and some not imaginable.

Increasingly, lines are blurring between the functions of police, military and intelligence. The CIA emphasizes military operations, while the Armed Forces take up spying. The distinction between the applications of these functions between domestic and overseas operations, and between citizen and non-citizen targets is likewise blurred.

There is also now a bewildering array of intelligence/military agencies operating in the U.S. and abroad. As many of the official services expand the scope of their activities, they turn to private contractors to do some of the tasks of the national security state. Coordinating what they all do, let alone attempting to contain it, is difficult and possibly futile. After the 9/11 attacks, a special commission pointed out this difficulty. As a result a new position and agency—the Director of National Intelligence in the Office of the National Counterintelligence Executive—was created to oversee much of this. Yet it would appear that especially the CIA, Department of Defense, FBI, and now Homeland security pursue their own agendas. Wikipedia has published a template of "Intelligence Agencies of the United States." They list the Central Intelligence Agency, Defense Intelligence Agency, National Security Agency, National Geospatial-Intelligence Agency, National Reconnaissance Office, Air Force Intelligence, Surveillance and Reconnaissance Office, Army Military Intelligence, Marine Corps Intelligence Activity, Office of Naval Intelligence, Coast Guard Intelligence, Federal Bureau of Investigation, Drug Enforcement Administration, Bureau of Intelligence and Research (State Dept.), Office of Intelligence and Analysis (Homeland Security Dept.), Office of Terrorism and

Financial Intelligence (Treasury Dept.), Office of Intelligence and Counterintelligence (Energy Dept.), Director of National Intelligence (Office of the National Counterintelligence Executive), Strategic Support Branch, National Clandestine Service, Defense Clandestine Service, National Counter-Proliferation Center, National Counterterrorism Center, President's Intelligence Advisory Board, Company Level Intelligence Cell and the Central Security Service.

I wonder if anyone, let alone any politically responsible leaders attempting to coordinate or establish limits, knows what all these agencies do? With the wide open legal/institutional framework for war and spying described earlier, there are many organizations equipped with the latest in spyware and lethal force capabilities. They have the potential for all sorts of abuses (as well as incompetence). We now take for granted the presence of searches at the airports, militarized borders, entrapment schemes that talk young self-professed radicals into trying to blow up bridges, people and infrastructure with fake bombs, grand jury investigations of political groups and spying on potential demonstrators. The Boston lockdown, and the drone attack and assassination of a U.S. teenager who, innocent of any terrorist leanings, was in Yemen looking for his father offer a glimpse of both present and future. As long as the U.S. attempts to hang onto a New World Order that has become a new world disorder, threats and attacks against the U.S. will continue, and the national security state will continue to evolve in response.

f. The Futile Search for Various "Best Practices"

There is no lack of good ideas for reforms that can make the new world disorder more orderly. I call all of these "best practices." Each of these could and have been analyzed in great detail. I will limit myself to citing some of them and commenting very briefly. My main points here are that the reforms I outline below are generally good ideas and should be tried. Each has groups and organizations trying to put them into practice. At the same time, it is crucial that we see these efforts in the context developed in this book.

The New World Order, which has become the new world disorder, came into being as a response to a *crisis of value*. And today we are experiencing yet another *crisis of value*. The very survival of today's form of global capitalism depends on many of the features that threaten its collapse. The present system, as I have stated, is one in which the U.S. is the dominant political, economic and military power, charged with the responsibility to protect and preserve the entire global system. It is a system where purchasing power depends on debt being a tradable commodity and where profit rates depend on producing value without adequately compensating the producers. Workers from Dhaka, Bangladesh to Sana, Yemen, from Karachi, Pakistan to Mogadishu, Somalia, and from Athens, Greece to Chicago, U.S.A are not getting enough of the value the system produces to live a decent life and in some cases to survive and reproduce. Environmental degradation, accelerated by the present system, can only be reversed by placing greater claims on the value the system is presently producing. And as the contradictions deepen, there is an insurgency from those not gaining the benefits of the system yet bearing its costs, which the U.S. military and intelligence apparatus is attempting to contain. *The implication for reforms and best practices is that they will at best be futile unless they stimulate a movement capable of challenging the New World Order itself.*

One source of tension in the system is the degree of inequality in the world, which heightens as the system falls into crisis. As discussed earlier, this is a common element of the entire global intifada. Entire nations are impoverished, as others seem wealthy by comparison. And within even the relatively wealthy nations there is an increasingly unequal distribution of wealth and income. There are some rather obvious remedies that can improve these disparities. Job development aimed at the unemployed and underemployed, job training, the poverty alleviation programs of agencies such as the World Bank, and tax policies within nations that place greater burdens on the wealthy than the poor are all examples. Such things ought to be done, but there are limits as long as the present system persists. A *crisis of value* means that there are greater claims on value than the system can possibly produce. This defines the limits of wealth and income distribution. Efforts can be made to reduce the claims made by the wealthy and increase those by the poor. But the wealthy, who run the system, will resist this and will agree with redistribution only to the extent that social movements threaten the viability of the system. Capitalists, moreover, need a certain amount of the value to invest in order to reproduce themselves and the system as a whole. So the needs of the system and the value it can generate define a limit on the redistribution of that value, no matter how strong social movements may become.

There is presently a reasonably strong environmental movement with an agenda aimed at limiting or even ending the environmental degradation discussed earlier. But these efforts have been just as strongly resisted. Efforts to limit the use of fossil fuels by enforcing regulations and developing cars and other machines that use less gas and oil, alternative energy source development, national carbon emissions standards, recycling, and even population controls have all been attempted to little effect and much resistance. The fact that the New World Order depends in part on higher levels of per capita consumption is a systemic dimension of environmental degradation. In addition, it is important to consider that any set of regulations that make private companies and citizens devote resources to reduce pollution of the environment are claims on value production. Since the crisis is a *crisis of value,* the amount of value relative to all claims on it places a limit on environmental cleanup.

There are also "best practices" or proposed practices designed to rein in the financial system. I mentioned earlier proposals for greater regulation of the activities of the derivatives markets. There have also been interesting proposals to tax transactions, imposing a cost on the trading of financial "products" that might limit that activity. In terms of international capital movement, the transactions tax might also be used to limit financial activities in other nations. In addition, many of the provisions of international trade agreements that limit the use of national capital controls could be reversed. "Fair trade" organizations have long supported the right of nations to exert various capital controls, such as requiring corporations doing business in a particular nation to put deposits in nationally based banks, and requiring that earnings stay in the country for a specified length of time. Also, it has been argued that "state-investor" rules, which enable corporations to sue nations for any practices that limit the profitability of their ventures (such as environmental regulations), should be repealed. There are presently "state-investor" rules in the North American

Free Trade Agreement and the World Trade Organization. Similar to measures to redistribute wealth, limitations on capital mobility have not only been fiercely resisted by investment banks and other types of corporations, but the activities to be reined-in were part of the "resolution" to the last crisis of value. They have become a critical aspect of the New World Order system. For these reasons, efforts to put brakes on the excesses of the finance industry are contradictory to the efforts by the U.S. Government and its corporations to hold on to the New World Order system.

A final set of reforms I consider here focus on local activism around housing and local economic development. In the 1990s, the growth of the New World Order system included a significant increase in housing prices due to the ready availability of mortgage funds, and rising incomes for a segment of the population considered to be at the top of the food chain. While that was going on, many working people found themselves either out of work or in jobs that paid a fraction of their previous wages. Also, public housing was being privatized.

One impact of these trends was that working class communities were invaded by emerging gentry who were building or rehabilitating existing homes that the working class and lower income residents couldn't afford. This generated a range of strategies on the part of not-for-profit community development corporations to preserve housing for the displaced working class. Community developers began to cobble together a number of government subsidies and programs. They assembled loans to build or rehabilitate existing housing to either sell or rent at more affordable prices. In some cases, subsidized funds were used to assemble tracts of land owned by the community development corporations—land trusts—that could be used for lower cost housing. The activity of putting together the financing was generally known as "loan packaging" or "doing deals" as community-based developers attempted to compete in the toxic world of real estate finance. There were some successes that benefited people of modest income. But when housing markets collapsed and there was still a shortage of jobs that paid enough to live a decent life, the limits to these practices turned out to be within the new world disorder itself.

Today, with most public housing demolished and a high incidence of evictions from homes bought with phantom funds generated by the housing derivatives markets, some of these ideas seem to be making a comeback. But as the New World Order crumbles into a new world disorder, community development schemes requiring even greater claims on value are even less viable than they were in the 1980s and 1990s. While a few families can and should be helped by these efforts, groups that are focused on affordable housing need to engage in a militant effort to block evictions and occupy foreclosed homes. Such militancy is at least questioning the systemic failures that make housing activism necessary.

These are the reasons why the efforts to fight for reforms of the existing system are futile in and of themselves. They should move forward if they can help people in dire circumstances, but activists need to consider the larger context of their work and use any momentum gained by implementing best practices to generate a movement for something new.

2. Challenges to U.S. Domination of Capitalism: A Multipolar World?

As the U.S. government and its corporations attempt to hang on to a New World Order in which the U.S. is the dominant player, there are other forces at work that also wish to maintain the present system, but diminish or eliminate U.S. power and control. This process is well under way at the present time. Some have predicted what they call a multipolar world. Clearly, simply changing leaders does nothing to address the crisis-ridden system we live in. But efforts to replace the U.S. as "the most powerful nation in the world" do explain many of the dimensions of today's global politics. For this reason I examine some of this dynamic below.

In looking at various aspects of the move to diminish or eliminate U.S. power in the world, we need to ask what exactly gives the U.S. its global dominance of the capitalist system. One aspect is the size of the U.S. economy. It is normally measured in terms of Gross Domestic Product (GDP), which is the sum of all consumer expenditures, private investment, government expenditures and net exports (the money value of exports minus imports). Much has been made of the fact that China's GDP is on track to overtake that of the U.S. But that's not all there is to it. The U.S. has used its status as the world's largest economy to dominate institutions like the International Monetary Fund and the World Bank, on which many nations depend. The size of both government and private investments has facilitated the development of new technologies that enable efficient and highly productive manufacturing, shipping and financial services. The size of domestic consumption in the U.S. makes it a key market for the products of nations worldwide. The replacement of U.S. economic power needs to address much more than simply GDP.

Military power is certainly another dimension of U.S. global dominance. As I discussed earlier, that dominance is being used to defend the New World Order system rather than simply the U.S. people. But as we have learned from the military failure of Vietnam, the attack on the World Trade Center, the spectacle of the militarization of greater Boston to subdue two young men who attacked the Boston Marathon, superior weapons do not guarantee U.S. supremacy. They can, in fact exacerbate the *crisis of value* that plagues U.S. society.

Within the context of a *crisis of value* that limits the effectiveness of both U.S. economic and military power, I have identified six ongoing efforts to diminish or displace U.S. dominance of the global capitalist system.

a. Can the "G's" Succeed Where U.S. Capital has Failed?

In 1975, as the Bretton Woods system was crumbling, the heads of state of the six wealthiest nations in the world met to discuss issues about how to preserve global capitalism and secure its economic future and military security. Many of the principles and broad provisions of the New World Order were hammered out in this meeting. The assembled nations called themselves the "Group of Six" or simply G6. Today the group continues to meet but includes two more nations so it is called G8. The original six included the U.S., France, Germany, Italy, Japan and England. Canada was added the following year, and in 1991, after the collapse of the Soviet Union, Russia made it 8. The European Union (EU) is also a member. "Wealthy" for the purposes of membership in this club is measured as the money value of assets such as real estate, stocks, technological achievements and education, minus debt liabilities. Essentially being "wealthy" means a nation's ability to take on debt and purchase goods and services, but it is also a measure of political and military power. The G8 holds an annual summit, but subgroups also meet regularly. Finance ministers of these nations and the EU meet four times a year to coordinate monetary policies.

As globalization connected to the New World Order has dispersed wealth and economic power even further, the significance and power of the G8 has declined. There is now a formation known as G8+5 that has added Brazil, China, India, Mexico and South Africa as special guests of this group. The five now attend G8 functions but many believe that another group known as the G20 is far more important than the G8 or the G8+5. The G20 consists of both the finance ministers and heads of state of 19 of the wealthiest nations plus the European Union. Its first summit was in 2008, and they continue to meet annually. Taken together, these nations account for over 80% of the world's gross domestic product (GDP), global trade, and growth. The U.S. continues to have significant power within these formations, all of which adhere to the neoliberal polices that constitute the New World Order.

The United Nations, through the UN Conference on Trade and Development (UNCTAD), formed its own "G" organization back in 1964. The point was and still is to get some of the least developed and poorest nations to form a bloc that can put forward its own agenda. It is known as G77. At a summit in Algiers in 1967, the G77 drew up a charter and formally constituted itself as an organization. It now has over 132 member nations, but the name G77 remains. Its purpose continues to be to form coalitions around strategies that will give the nation members more leverage in deliberations with the United Nations. In 1971, a subcommittee of G77 calling itself G24 formed to focus on monetary and development finance issues. The G24 is closely tied to the policies of the International Monetary Fund (IMF), and thus the U.S. dominated neoliberal policies and programs of the global capitalist system.

All of these "G" formations are dedicated to pursue U.S. dominated neoliberal policies. For this reason, it seems unlikely that they could be a viable alternative to U.S. political power over the entire system. Also, there are significant political divisions within each bloc and within nations over how the New World Order system should be applied to them. So as the *crisis of value* continues to deepen, it seems unlikely that these groups could be a basis for a multipolar world.

b. The European Union and Monetary Union

As the European Union (EU) evolved, and after many of its nations formed a monetary union that replaced their individual currencies with the Euro, some predicted that Europe could replace the U.S. as the leader of the New World Order. A great deal has been written about the EU. I used to devote half of an entire course to it. Here, I will just skim the surface to explain why I don't believe the EU is likely to replace the U.S. as the leader of the new world disorder. If readers want to go more deeply into this subject, a good start would be the article in Wikipedia that has a ton of references and bibliography. (htpp//.en.wikipedia.org/wiki/European_Union)

After World War II, with Europe a shambles, the leaders of six European nations began to hold talks to find a basis for European unity that could prevent future disastrous wars among them. The objective was to create a common market so Europeans could share their resources and talents. A united Europe would promote the free movement of people, goods, services and capital within the region.

The venture began modestly, in 1950, with the formation of a common market for steel and coal among the original six nations known as the European Coal and Steel Community. Over the years, new treaties, new members and new communities and activities were added. Individual national passports were eliminated. In 1993, the association was named the European Union; its charter contained institutions that governed 27 nations. In 1999, seventeen of these nations formed a monetary union by eliminating their own currencies and adopting the Euro as their common currency.

The EU presently includes a number of governmental institutions. The European Council and European Commission function as an executive, proposing legislation and administering EU programs. There is a parliament that debates and decides on legislation. There is a European court and a central bank. The difference between the EU and a national government is that while nations govern relations and activities of its people and corporations, the EU governs relations among the nations who are members.

The EU's budget is funded by contributions from member nations assessed by formulas laid out in the EU charter. About two-thirds of EU revenues are a percentage of the gross national income of each nation. Also, revenues are a percentage of a common "value added tax" (a special type of sales tax) raised by all nations. The EU has no independent taxing authority, and efforts to make all revenue gathering uniform within nations across the EU have been resisted. Most of the spending by the EU has been devoted to agriculture (47%) and programs geared to the economic development within regions of Europe (30%). These programs, known as structural funds, are geared to reducing inequalities in income, wealth, and employment opportunity within the region. In the past, Portugal, Ireland, Greece, and Spain (PIGS) have received the greatest share of the structural funds.

Recently, as the crisis of value has deepened, the EU system has been seriously challenged. The PIGS nations in particular have been hit so hard that unemployment has reached catastrophic levels. At the time of this writing, the average unemployment rate for all 27 EU nations is 12.2% (in the U.S. on this date the rate was 7.6%). The rate is much higher in PIGS nations. In Spain, the unemployment rate is 26.8%, in Portugal 17.8%, Greece 27%, Ireland, 12.3%. In some countries the rate for youth is higher yet: 24.4% for the entire EU area, Spain 55.2%, Portugal 38.4%, Greece 57.9%, Ireland 29.4%. These nations, which earlier received structural funds for development from the EU, seem to be in the worst trouble. But a number of EU nations are doing better. Germany's rate is the lowest, at 4.1%, though rates generally are on the rise. France has recently slumped into official recession. Loans to resolve debt and budget crises from the EU bank come with conditions attached which amount to extreme austerity. There are cuts on social and government spending when it is most needed for relief and job development. The result is predictable; many Europeans are in the streets protesting. And the disparities between especially Germany and the rest of Europe are not going unnoticed. Nationalism appears to be on the rise in some quarters and old resentments toward Germany, which is pushing the austerity programs, simmer. (www.ec.europa.eu/eurostat)

The EU enterprise depends on a willingness of nations to give up a certain amount of their sovereignty and tax revenues for the sake of the entire region. It is based on the notion that if everyone chips in to help the poorer nations in the union, everyone will be better off. But as a *crisis of value* deepens, these ideals are likely to go out the window. Helping Greece will not help Germany. Helping Ireland will not help the United Kingdom. The solutions being pushed by Germany are meant to preserve the new world disorder. Not only will this not resolve the crisis, it makes the EU an unlikely candidate to displace the U.S. as the leader of this mess.

c. A Second Coming of Simon Bolivar

In 1813, Simon Bolivar, who was born in Caracas, Venezuela, led an armed struggle for independence from Spain. In doing so he united forces in a region called Gran Columbia that encompassed what is today Venezuela, Columbia, Panama, Ecuador, Peru, Bolivia and portions of Brazil. The Spanish were defeated in 1919. Bolivar envisioned a new nation modeled after the United States of America—a United States of Latin America. He remained in power from1819 until 1830 when rivalries among what are today different nations broke the republic apart.

In 1999, Venezuela elected Hugo Chavez president by a 56% majority over four other candidates. He held this margin throughout four presidential terms. Chavez attempted to reignite Bolivar's vision by holding a constitutional convention and renaming his nation "The Bolivarian Republic of Venezuela." His words and actions clearly expressed his intent to rid Latin America of U.S. domination.

To further this vision Chavez played a leading role in organizing regional institutions that could form an economic and political bloc. In 2004, Chavez signed an agreement with Cuba to trade oil for health care. This enabled Venezuela to construct and staff many health clinics for the poor and to train a new generation of physicians. By 2009, this had evolved into the Bolivarian Alliance for the Peoples of Our Americas (ALBA), which offered a number of programs for regional cooperation, mutual aid and trade. In addition to Venezuela and Cuba, members include Ecuador, Bolivia, Nicaragua, Dominica, Antiqua/Barbuda, St. Vincent and the Grenadines, while Haiti, Iran and Syria have been invited as observers. A major spinoff of ALBA is a central Bank of the South that has established a common electronic currency (Sucre) that is used for trade purposes as a partial monetary union. Chavez also established a regional satellite television station called TeleSUR in 2005.

Finally, a treaty signed in 2008 established the Union of South American Nations (UNASUR) that included Argentina, Bolivia, Brazil Chile, Columbia, Ecuador, Guyana, Paraguay, Peru, Suriname, Uruguay, and Venezuela. Panama and Mexico are listed as observers. UNASUR has established a common market for trade without tariffs and free movement of peoples across borders. It has established an electoral monitoring agency to replace the U.S. dominated Organization of American States (OAS), a mutual security agreement and an infrastructure development program that includes energy development. UNASUR presently seems to be moving in the direction of becoming a South American counterpart of the EU. It is not likely to take power from the U.S. anytime soon but is limiting U.S. domination.

The policies of the South American nations that make up ALBA and UNASUR vary. A number of them depart from the neoliberal policies of the New World Order but remain capitalist. Chavez has used oil revenues for social development that have raised large numbers of people out of poverty and illiteracy.

d. China and the BRICS Alliance

In 2009, the heads of state of Brazil, Russia, India and China (BRIC) held a summit in Russia to discuss how an alliance among these four nations could promote economic cooperation for their mutual benefit. They also discussed how such cooperation could help developing nations in general. And they called for the formation of a new global reserve currency (discussed below) to replace the domination of the U.S. dollar. The following year they met again, adding South Africa to the group, and changed their name to BRICS. Each nation originally pledged funds to bolster the U.S. dominated International Monetary Fund (IMF) but in 2013 they decided to form their own development bank that could rival IMF.

BRICS nations account for 25% of the world economy (measured in terms of GDP) and 40% of the world's population. In addition to the formation of a BRICS development bank, the alliance signed agreements specifying that $500 billion worth of trade would be transacted using their own currencies, rather than the dollar, as common currency. They also created a think tank to do research and come up with possible joint development projects. A business council involving 900 business professionals was formed to promote private joint ventures. BRICS meets annually. In 2013 they met in Durban, South Africa, where the focus was on developing the BRICS Bank as well as on how BRICS could invest in the nations of the African Continent with South Africa as a "gateway."

BRICS has recently completed the construction of an alternative Internet infrastructure that is free of U.S. control and involvement. In the wake of revelations about U.S. spying on Brazil through the Internet, President Dilma Rousseff announced that Brazil was divorcing itself from the "U.S.-centric Internet." It will no longer entrust data to U.S. companies like Facebook and Google, which have been penetrated by the U.S. National Security Agency. Instead, Brazil plans to move its Internet use to the alternative BRICS structure.

Except for the fact that both China and Russia have a relatively large government sector, all the BRICS nations have been moving steadily in the direction of the neoliberal policies of the New World Order. The challenge they pose is not primarily to the New World Order system itself but rather to the U.S.'s dominating role. But even this challenge is weakened by contradictions and conflict among its members and in relation to other nations. BRICS itself is dominated by China. China's economy in terms of GDP accounts for 55% of the total GDP of the five nations. Its GDP is four times greater than the next largest economy, Brazil. China's exports account for 63% of the total and represent 85% of BRICS trade. Thus China is in a position to dictate BRICS policies, and is likely to do so for its own benefit. Moreover, China, Russia and India are competing to dominate Asia and that seems to include an arms race in their mutual border areas. These factors limit the possibility of an alliance strong enough to dislodge the U.S. as the dominant force in the New World Order. And as the *crisis of value* deepens and impacts these economies further, they will be weakened to the same degree as the U.S. and Europe. That leaves the question about the ultimate potential of China itself.

Many people believe that of all the nations in the world, China is most likely to replace the U.S. as the leader of the New World Order. In *When China Rules the World* (2011, Penguin Books), author Martin Jacques makes a strong case for this possibility. A number of forecasters believe that the growth of China's economy, measured in terms of gross domestic product (GDP), is on a trajectory to overtake the U.S. in the next decade. Furthermore, China is making strategic loans, investments and alliances that suggest that the nation is positioning itself to strengthen its economy enough to play a leadership role in the world. A rather contemptuous article in the *New York Times* (Heriberto Araújo, & Juan Pablo Cardenal, June 2, 2013: China's Economic Empire) refers to China as a "state capitalist" nation they term "China, Inc." They point out that Chinese capitalists are forced to put their savings into Chinese state banks that pay little or no interest. The government and its government enterprises can draw on these savings to make strategic loans and to invest not only in China, but also in nations around the world. Many political leaders in the U.S. and the media have expressed fear over the fact that China is a major lender to the U.S., buying government bonds. But its lending activity goes much further. According to the *New York Times* report, between 2009 and 2010 China was the largest lender in the world. Its loans to other nations that year amounted to $110 billion—greater than those of the World Bank.

Most important for China's position in the world and its own future development, are its loans, foreign investments and trade agreements in the developing world. China needs three things to continue its own development: a number of natural resources, energy and food. Loan, investment and trade policies are directed toward gaining the resources and food commodities it needs while also gaining political influence. Jacques points to the fact that in the year 2001, China launched its "going global" strategy. This resulted in a sharp increase in overseas investments, loans, and a flurry of trade agreements and economic alliances such as BRICS. The *New York Times* analysis demonstrates that top lending and investment destinations include Venezuela, Iran, Angola, Myanmar, Cambodia, Ecuador, Zambia, Sudan and Zimbabwe. In many cases, repayments of loans are made in resources such as oil, gas, minerals and food commodities. Investments have focused on energy, such as oil pipelines and refinement facilities as well as hydroelectric dams. China has become the leading trading partner in Tajikistan, Turkmenistan, Kyrgyzstan, Australia, Iran, Angola, Japan, South Korea and Chile. It is the second leading trade partner with Kazakhstan, Uzbekistan, Guinea, Saudi Arabia, Brazil, Peru, Venezuela and South Africa. Nearly all of this trade is focused on energy and food. China is also involved in a variety of multinational economic alliances that include not only trade but also agreements involving investment, immigration, and security.

In addition to the BRICS, China's most significant multilateral association is the Shanghai Cooperation Organization (SCO), which has stated its intention of preventing U.S. domination of the region, as defined by its member nations. SCO was founded in 2001 and consists of China, Russia, Uzbekistan, Kazakhstan, Tajikistan and Kyrgyzstan—they share common borders. During their annual summits, a number of other nations have been granted observer status, while still others have applied for and received recognition as "dialogue partners." The present observer nations are Afghanistan, India, Pakistan, Iran, and Mongolia. Dialogue partners include Belarus, Sri Lanka and Turkey. Turkey has indicated that if it could become a full member of SCO it would give up its membership application to the European Union. That request was rejected. The U.S. applied for observer status in 2006 and was rejected. SCO has a formal structure and a number of cooperative programs. These include military cooperation that involves intelligence sharing, counterterrorism programs and some joint military exercises. There are also joint energy and resource agreements that include oil, gas, hydrocarbon reserves and the joint use of water. China has extended special loans to members from less-developed countries. The SCO is exploring the possibility of establishing a free trade zone and a regional banking system that would include Iran.

Despite these impressive moves on the part of China and other nations in the BRICS and SCO, the success of China's ambition to lead the New World Order, is far from certain. For one thing, China's economic growth now depends on exporting consumer goods and machinery to the rest of the world. Exports dominate China's GDP. Domestic consumption is very low. (By contrast, 2/3 of GDP in the U.S. is domestic consumption and a very small portion is exports.) To maintain economic growth based on a dominant export sector requires China to be competitive by paying low wages, it requires a flow of resources and foreign investment to be able to produce goods locally, and it requires the maintenance of large overseas markets. These conditions may not be sustainable. It is also important to note that China's loans to the U.S. must be maintained, and even expanded, in order for people in the U.S. to buy Chinese goods. If we did not buy Chinese products it would threaten China's export sector and compromise economic growth.

The low wages and poor working conditions needed to produce cheap products and to make China attractive to foreign investors are causing labor unrest. Low wages also contribute to the inequities within the nation that not only cause unrest but keep it from building a stronger domestic consumption sector. Also, China lacks sufficient energy and minerals to maintain its high rate of economic growth. For example, China is only able to produce 4 million barrels of oil per day domestically, while it uses 8.2 million. It must then use its surplus to invest in oil and minerals overseas, which can crowd out domestic investment. Furthermore, there are high environmental costs to China's rapid industrial development. Water quality is bad throughout the country. Solid waste disposal is a huge problem. Air quality is terrible in most industrial cities, and China's growth of industry is contributing greatly to the greenhouse gasses that lead to global warming. Finally, there is a real problem with food security. Only 15% of the land in China is capable of producing food. And much of the area suitable for food production is also the area where rapid industrialization has been taking place. All of these factors suggest that there is no certainty that China is on a path to "ruling the world."

e. The Status of the U.S. Dollar

China, as well as a number of other nations, has been taking steps to become independent of the U.S. dollar in international trade and finance endeavors. There is also some discussion of creating an alternative to the dollar's status as "global reserve currency." Losing that status could have a serious impact on the ability of the U.S. to dominate the New World Order, and will have serious repercussions for the domestic economy of the U.S. and the entire New World Order system. For that reason I now turn to the questions: What does "global reserve currency" mean? And how does this status for the dollar contribute to U.S. power in the world capitalist system?

Presently there are global markets for the currencies of different nations. There are several reasons why nations and private investors buy foreign currencies and hold some of them in reserve. One reason involves international trade in goods and services. When a nation imports goods and services from other nations, they have to pay for them in the national currency of the nation where the goods are produced. For example, if people in China want to buy a Chevy SUV, the Chinese dealer who buys the car has to pay in dollars. If they want Toyotas, they have to pay Japan in yen. The car dealer would go to their bank and cash in renminbi for dollars and yen. To cover transactions such as these and other global financial transactions, banks hold "foreign reserve currencies," meaning they can be used directly to settle trade accounts or be easily converted to other currencies. Generally, the foreign exchange reserves amount to about three month's worth of trade.

There are other reasons for holding foreign reserve currencies. When a central bank prints and circulates money, it represents a promise that the money will buy goods and services once the money is circulated. Money, of course, allows people to buy and sell the goods and services they need. But its use is based on a promise from the government. That promise is therefore a liability that prudent governments cover with an asset. The asset in international finance and trade is the currencies of other governments. Government central banks hold reserves of foreign currencies that can be used for trade as well as a guarantee of their own currency. The most widely held foreign reserve currency is the dollar. This is what's meant by the dollar having "global reserve currency" status.

The front of a U.S. dollar bill reads, "Federal Reserve Note, The United States of America, and One Dollar," On the back it adds, "In God We Trust." A British five-pound bill has a picture of the Queen and says "Bank of England. I promise to pay the bearer on demand the sum of five pounds." Trust in God or the Queen aside, somehow the government has to make good on it. The status of the U.S. dollar and the British pound as global reserve currencies means that most of the world has enough faith in them that they are willing to accept them as assets in their central banks. But the fact that most local currencies are considered liabilities can be illustrated by the case of Zimbabwe.

In 1980, the apartheid government of Rhodesia was overthrown and became Zimbabwe. The Rhodesian dollar was exchanged for a new currency, the Zimbabwe dollar, on a one to one basis. But years of war and exploitation meant that the economy was in shambles. There were shortages of basic goods and services that led to high rates of inflation. Soon, it took so many Zimbabwe dollars to buy anything that they devalued them (made them worth less) and reprinted each dollar with a bigger number on it. This happened over and over again. Eventually, notes were printed that said, "I promise to pay the bearer on demand, one hundred trillion dollars from the Reserve Bank of Zimbabwe." Ironically, there is a picture of a male cape buffalo (bull) on the bill. Ultimately Zimbabwe simply agreed to let people transact business in any currency they could get their hands on. Zimbabwe also lacks foreign reserve currencies, which limits their ability to engage in trade or even attract foreign investment. (While traveling in Zimbabwe, an innkeeper gave me a hundred trillion dollar note as a souvenir. The *Wall Street Journal* later reported that these are now worth five American dollars as collectables!)

Nations try to hold foreign exchange reserves in currencies that can be used in trade or considered assets to offset their own currency. Central banks of large economies hold a reserve of different currencies that have global reserve status. However, they select one currency, based on their assessment of the size and stability of the economy it represents, and hold most of their "foreign exchange reserves" in that currency. In the case of the U.S. dollar, holdings are not simply in treasury notes like dollar bills but in dollar denominated assets like government short- term notes and longer-term bonds. The U.S. sells its debt in the form of bonds and notes in global markets where they are purchased by governments and private investors.

The International Monetary Fund has collected data on the distribution of foreign exchange reserves since 1958. Presently the U.S. dollar dominates reserves, accounting for about 62% of the reserves held by most of the nations in the world. The Euro comes in second at 24%. The British pound and the Japanese yen are next at about 4% each. The Chinese renminbi cannot have this status because the Chinese government controls the flow of capital in and out of the country—there is no guarantee of its convertibility or a market mechanism to determine its exchange rate (more on exchange rates later).

As discussed earlier, the dollar was declared the global reserve currency under the terms of the 1947 Bretton Woods Agreement. The U.S. Government backed its dollars with gold; the price of gold relative to the dollar was fixed. That changed in 1971 when President Nixon declared that the dollar was no longer exchangeable for gold. In 1973, he also announced that the value of the dollar in relation to other currencies was no longer fixed. Exchange rates were then set by buying and selling various currencies in international markets. Nonetheless, the world continued to trade in dollars and to hold them as foreign exchange currency. That status continues today, but is being challenged.

The status of the dollar as the global reserve currency is critically important to the U.S. economy and the entire New World Order system. The U.S. Federal Reserve Bank engages in the buying and selling of foreign currencies. They do so for purposes of foreign trade and to influence the dollar value of other currencies. But the assets they hold are generally denominated in U.S. dollars. The Federal Reserve buys U.S. government debt and holds that as a reserve. They can only do this because the global reserve status of the dollar guarantees that there will always be a demand for dollars. This enables the U.S. to essentially treat its own currency as an asset, rather than a liability. The U.S. government is thus able to finance its debt by selling dollar denominated bonds and notes not only to the Federal Reserve Bank, but also to other governments and private investors. Selling U.S. Government debt is just like printing money. The difference between a thousand dollar's worth of twenty-year government bonds and a thousand dollars in cash is this: The cash can be used immediately to buy goods and services, while the bonds would have to be sold for cash or cashed in after twenty years. The bonds also earn interest and generate more cash. Not only does the guaranteed demand for dollars enable the U.S. to sell its debt, it can also print money. Yet all of this is contingent on the faith investors and governments have in the viability of the U.S. economy and its stability.

If there was no demand for dollars internationally, the U.S. would be much more restricted in borrowing and determining the supply of its money. Since the present New World Order depends on debt as a commodity, challenges to the dollar's status could seriously compromise the ability of the U.S. government, households, and private companies to use debt and various fictitious products to prop up the ability of people and our government to spend and consume.

There is one further aspect of the status of the U.S. Dollar that contributes to U.S. domination of global capitalism, and that is its exchange rate. The functioning of the New World Order depends in part on the ability of U.S. consumers to purchase goods in the wake of the attack on wages that occurred when U.S. manufacturing moved overseas. As discussed earlier, part of this was accomplished by running up household and mortgage debt and selling it in global markets. But in addition, products once produced in the U.S. need to be cheaper when they are produced in other nations and affordable to low wage workers when they are imported into the U.S. Cheap products made in China, Vietnam or Bangladesh sold at Walmart are cheap not only because of low wages and poor working conditions in those countries, but also because of the exchange rate between the dollar and their currencies.

So, how many euros, renminbis/yuan, dong, or takas will a U.S. dollar buy and what difference does it make? There are plenty of currency converters on the Internet that answer the first question. As I write this, a dollar is only "worth" .77 euros. But you can exchange a dollar for 6.16 Chinese yuan, 20,915 Vietnamese dong, and 78.12 Bangladesh takas. As you read this, the rates will quite likely be different. If you tracked exchange rates over a period of time you would see that they are in a constant state of flux. This is because there is a global market for currencies in which national central banks, as well as other banks and investors, buy and sell on a regular basis. In the short term this buying and selling alters exchange rates. Through its central bank, the Chinese government can and does buy lots of U.S. dollars in exchange for yuan, which keeps the value of the yuan low in dollar terms. The U.S. Federal Reserve also plays this game and can "strengthen" (keep the price of the dollar in other currencies high) or "weaken" the U.S. dollar. The European Union and the British can do the same.

There is a standard that gives some idea of whether currencies are exchanging above or below where they should be. It is called "Purchasing Power Parity" or PPP. Often PPP is used to compare international financial data (such as Gross Domestic Product) in different countries. It converts financial data into a single currency, usually $PPP. It can also be used as a measure of long-term exchange rates. Purchasing Power Parity takes the price of a group of goods in a specific country in its own currency and compares it to the price of the same goods in a different country in its own currency. The ratio between the two prices is then used as the PPP exchange rate between the two currencies. For example, if you look at the price of a Big Mac in yen in Tokyo and dollars in

David Ranney

New York, that should give you the "real" exchange rate. In fact, the *Economist Magazine* regularly publishes a "Big Mac Index" of exchange rates. PPP is a much more complex measure that takes "market baskets" of goods that are frequently purchased in the different countries whose currencies are being compared. If we want a PPP exchange rate between U.S. dollars and yen, the PPP market basket might include everything from Big Macs to Toyotas.

Nations are forever accusing one another of manipulating the "value" of their currencies. Right now it is fashionable in the U.S. to accuse both China and Japan of keeping the yuan and yen too low relative to the dollar. Since 1973, virtually all nations engaged in trade and buying and selling securities like U.S. bonds and notes have attempted to manipulate currency exchange rates. They do so for two reasons. China and Japan wish to "weaken" the yuan and yen (make them cheaper relative to the U.S. dollar and other currencies) so their exports will be cheaper on foreign markets. This will make American consumers buy Toyotas and cheap Chinese clothes at Walmart rather than more expensive items made in the USA. The other form of manipulation is to "strengthen" a currency to facilitate investments overseas or enhance the sale of securities. In reality, it is difficult to judge charges of manipulation. The PPP measure itself can be manipulated by altering what goods and services are included in any given "market basket." It is easy for nations or people to disagree on whether or not a country is manipulating.

Since the 1970s and until the last few years, the U.S. has had a policy of "keeping the dollar strong." This damaged markets for U.S. exports because it made them more expensive in nations with weaker currencies. But a strong dollar made U.S. bonds and other dollar denominated assets like mortgage-backed securities very marketable overseas. Because the U.S. and capitalism in general were deliberately encouraging our export industries to ship to low wage countries, and were trying to run the world by trading in dollar-denominated debt like bonds and mortgages, there was little concern about the collapse of export markets. But with the present *crisis of value*, U.S. policy makers are in the clutches of a contradiction. Debt still needs to be highly marketable, but the U.S. also needs to increase export markets to create jobs at home. Furthermore, persistent and growing trade imbalances (imports greater than exports) act as a drag on economic growth.

Maintaining the dollar as the global reserve currency is a key aspect of U.S. dominance of the global capitalist New World Order. It not only enables the U.S. and the entire system to run on the phantasm of debt as a commodity, but it also gives the U.S. a greater ability to manipulate exchange rates. The dollar is still dominant at 62% of all foreign exchange reserves. But keep in mind that right after the Bretton Woods Agreement was signed, it was the *only* reserve currency. Even after Nixon's withdrawal of the gold standard and the opening up of global currency markets, the dollar was still as high as 85%. Between 1958 and 1995 it fell to 58%. In 1996 it began to rise again, and in 2000 reached a high of 71% before steadily falling to its present 62%. (International Monetary Fund's *Composition of Foreign Exchange Reserves Series* or COFER www.imf.org)

These declines represent the estimates of other national central banks of the viability of the U.S. economy as well as their efforts to diminish dependence on the dollar. At one point many nations, particularly those in Europe, believed the euro could potentially replace the dollar as the dominant reserve currency. As the global crisis hits Europe, this seems no longer likely. In fact, the future of the euro itself is in question.

Other nations are attempting to reduce dependence on the dollar for both trade and investment. One approach involves bilateral (two nation) trade agreements in which each nation accepts the other's currency. Such an agreement, for example, was signed between Brazil and Russia in March 2013. This means that over half of all of the trade between these two nations will not use U.S. dollars or any other foreign exchange currency. Another approach to diminishing dependence on the dollar involves trade alliances that create a special trade currency. This currency is then interchangeable, at an agreed upon rate, with the currencies of all the nations in the alliance. The Bolivarian Alliance of the Americas (ALBA), discussed earlier, has eliminated use of the dollar in their alliance. Instead, they have created another currency, the sucre. They all trade with one another in sucres, which are exchangeable for the currencies of member nations.

A third approach that can contribute to diminishing the U.S. dollar's status as a global reserve currency has been to create regional development banks that are free of U.S. involvement. The policies of the International Monetary Fund (IMF) and the World Bank are controlled by the U.S. and depend on U.S. dollars to operate. Emerging regional development banks are an alternative to IMF and World Bank. Banco del Sur (Bank of the South) was established in 2009 by Argentina, Brazil, Paraguay, Uruguay, Ecuador, Bolivia and Venezuela. At the time of this writing it is not yet operational, but its founders have indicated that it soon will be. A similar bank is under development by the BRICS. These banks will not avoid using U.S. dollars altogether, but development policies will be independent of the U.S.

It is fair to say that the status of the U.S. dollar as the global reserve currency is still quite solid. And that won't change over night. However, the emergence of trade agreements and development banks that offer an alternative to the dollar suggest that its status in the world is being challenged. If the dollar should lose its global dominance it would greatly diminish U.S. domination over global capitalism. It would also diminish the ability of the U.S. to sell its debt and dollar denominated assets. Since U.S. government and household debt sold in global markets is at the heart of the New World Order, this is a challenge both to U.S. dominance of global capitalism and to the present system through which capitalism functions. But this does not challenge capitalism itself—there is always the possibility of a "newer world order."

3. Prospects For A Newer World Order: Today's *Extractivism*

Capitalist crises of value in the past have always resulted in some new form of capitalism. In the late 1940s it was the Bretton Woods system. In the 1980s it was the New World Order. In each of these cases there was a wholesale destruction of claims on value. The U.S., with economic and military power, was ready to take the reins and mold a new form of capitalism to fit the needs and capacity of its government and its corporations. At these historical moments it was not clear what the outcome would be. During the period from 1960-80 there was no universal understanding that we were facing a crisis of value, and that the collapse of manufacturing in the industrial nations—especially the U.S.—and its emergence in low-wage nations would constitute wholesale destruction of claims on value. Nor did we understand how profoundly changed the capitalist system that emerged in the mid 1980s really was. Today, we are in a similar state of confusion. We are in the very early stage of a crisis. It is difficult to say with certainty what a new form of capitalism could possibly look like. Neither is it possible to say whether or not capitalism will continue to exist at all. One possibility, though, is that capitalism will prevail, as it has in the past, but that it will take a new form.

A new form of capitalism requires that claims on value generated in the New World Order be destroyed and a new system for creating and accumulating surplus values be put into place. When the New World Order was established, it meant specifically that manufacturing in industrial nations, particularly in the U.S., was destroyed and moved to lower wage areas. Surplus value through industrial production was then replaced with a fictitious or phantom commodity: debt. The financial collapse and massive foreclosures that followed are the beginning of the destruction of claims on value today. There is some movement in the direction of finding a new source of value and surplus accumulation. Whether this movement evolves into a new form of capitalism remains to be seen, but it's worth taking a look at it in its present state.

Some activists are calling this development "extractivism." To understand this concept it is useful to look at a similar development that marked the beginnings of capitalism itself. As noted earlier, capitalism in Europe replaced a system of feudalism in the 19th Century. At that time, large numbers of wage laborers had to be found who would produce more value than they received in wages. It also required a source of wealth that could be used to build factories, tools, and machines. But where did these wage laborers come from in the beginning? And where did the original capitalists get the wealth that was needed? Classical economist Adam Smith put a positive spin on what he called "primitive accumulation," saying that some people just worked harder than others and had more as a result. So they simply hired those who had less. Later, Karl Marx developed a very different explanation. He pointed out that peasants who had access to common land were forcibly separated from it, which impoverished them and gave them no option but to work for capitalists. The new class of capitalists had gained their newfound wealth by taking it from the colonies, including America. Marx put it this way:

> "The capitalist system pre-supposes the complete separation of the laborers from all property and the means by which they can realize their labor...The so-called primitive accumulation, therefore, is nothing else than the historical process of divorcing the producer from the means of production." (Karl Marx (1867), *Capital*, Vol I , ch. xxvi)

He goes on to document the legal and military process in which feudal lords with sufficient monetary wealth drove the peasants from common lands and turned those lands into private property. And where did that monetary wealth come from?

> "The discovery of gold and silver in America, the extirpation, enslavement and entombment in mines of the aboriginal populations, the beginning of the conquest and looting of the East Indies, the turning of Africa into a warren for the commercial hunting of black skins, signalized the rosy dawn of the era of capitalist production. These idyllic proceedings are the chief

momenta of primitive accumulation." (Karl Marx (1867), *Capital*, Vol. I, Ch. XXXI)

So what does this have to do with what is going on today, and how does this offer some insight into the prospects for a new form of capitalism that could emerge from the ultimate collapse of the New World Order? First of all, a number of writers since Marx have noted that primitive accumulation didn't simply stop with the establishment of the capitalist system. Primitive accumulation goes side by side with the dominant form of accumulation, such as the New World Order. David Harvey, for example, makes this point in his book *The New Imperialism* (2003). He even gives the concept a different name, calling it "accumulation though dispossession." I agree with this but make an additional point that many of today's challenges to U.S. domination of the New World Order and to the system itself are building on activities that look a lot like what Marx called primitive accumulation.

At the World Social Forum held in Tunis in March of 2013, an international group of activists held a panel on a process they called *extractivism*.

They warn about a:

"global extractivist boom that is leading to great misery for many hundreds of millions of the Earth's people and destroying the very basis for life and its reproduction...expanding capital's reach and destroying our common goods of water, land, air, forests and oceans." (Extractives Assembly, Political Declaration, World Social Forum, Tunis, Algeria, March 31, 2003)

They go on to note:

"International financial institutions are encouraging extractivism as the major engine to fuel economic growth... (They) are looking for new areas for... financialised forms of profit making, with natural resource extraction representing a site for rapid and substantial accumulation...Extractivism is characterized by intertwined collusion between state and corporations...Extractivism is resulting in the displacement of peasant, indigenous people and rural populations, as land is grabbed for mining, oil extraction, plantations and dams...Water theft accompanies..."

This statement at the World Social Forum was preceded by a meeting in Durban, South Africa, in February of 2013, held to protest a meeting of the BRICS in that same city. Most of those attending were activists and researchers who had been fighting various forms of extractivism around the world, but particularly in Africa involving land grabs, dam construction, oil extraction and fracking. According to counter-conference organizer Patrick Bond, the BRICS were meeting in South Africa "to assure the rest of Africa that their countries' corporations are better investors in infrastructure, mining, oil and agriculture than the traditional European and U.S. multinationals." But the counter-conference, called "BRICS from Below," offered a stinging critique of BRICS participation in using land grabs, dams, oil mining and other extractive investments to further the interests of multinational financial and industrial corporations that would impoverish millions of people.

David Ranney

Patrick Bond published a special reader for the occasion called "BRICS in Africa: Anti-Imperialist, Sub-Imperialist, or In Between?" (www.ukzn.ac.za/files/bond) CCS Booklet 22 March 2013.pdf) One of the papers: "BRICS Grab African Land and Sovereignty," by Tomaso Ferrando, argues that "land grabbing" is a global phenomenon that impacts access to land and water affecting seven billion people "whose food security is everyday more at risk." Ferrando writes, "Land grabbing is bad not only because it takes the land away, but also because it implements an economic model which is socially, economically, politically and ethically unsustainable and unacceptable." Many nations in the global south have huge tracts of land that lack titles and technically belong to the state. But they are lands that are utilized for the subsistence of people and contain waterways essential to life on the land.

Increasingly, governments of many of the nations challenging U.S. hegemony over the New World Order are negotiating bilateral trade agreements (BITS) that facilitate the sale of these lands to other nations such as China, or to global investors. According to Ferrando, the number of BITS is exploding. Only 400 were signed between 1959 and 1991. But by 2008, the number had risen to 2600, and China has been involved in 60% of them. Most African nations have constitutional provisions, which state that non-titled land belongs to the public, nation, or some institutionalized authority. The authorities are allowed to manage the land but not to dispose of it, but the government does have the power to dispose of its national resources. The BITS contracts define land as a natural resource open to foreign investors. They are reminiscent of the 18th and 19th Century English Enclosure Acts that turned over what had once been common lands used by peasants for grazing, mowing hay and growing crops to large landholders who then expelled the peasants from these lands. This was a significant part of the "rosy dawn" of the capitalist system. The result of today's BITS contracts, according to Ferrando, is that "millions of people have already been displaced or prevented from accessing their traditional land under the cover of a complex legal network formed by contract, national, international and investment law." He cites research by the International Land Coalition that states that 200 million hectares (494 million acres) have been transferred by similar land grabbing around the world.

BRICS nations are heavily involved in land grabbing not only in Africa but in Southeast Asia and South America as well. Ferrando cites data from the International Land Coalition, Oxfam and Land Matrix initiative that show that China has purchased nearly 3 million acres of these lands throughout Africa, South America and in China itself. A great deal of China's industrial development separated peasants from lands capable of producing food in favor of factories, turning peasants into the new industrial working class. India has taken 4.4 million acres of peasant lands in its own nation and throughout Southeast Asia, Eastern, Central and Northern Africa. Brazil has taken lands in East Africa but is also participating in the destruction of Amazon rain forests. They have failed to recognize claims and rights to lands there by a substantial movement of "peoples without lands." South Africa has participated in land grabs to the tune of 3.4 million acres.

China is also a major player in building dams that take lands and divert water used for farming and fishing. China's Three Gorges Dam is the largest hydroelectric plant in the world. Further, a recent *New York Times* study (June 2, 2013) published a world map that locates Chinese-funded dam projects. Those already constructed are located in Vietnam, Laos, Cambodia, The Philippines, Malaysia, Myanmar, Pakistan, Nepal, Russia, thirteen nations on the African Continent, five nations of Central Asia, Ecuador, Venezuela and Honduras. I counted a total of 113 dams built in the past ten years and at least that many more proposed.

In addition to the BRICS, many other nations that are contesting U.S. power are doing so using one form or another of *extractivism*, or what Adam Smith and Karl Marx both called primitive accumulation. Bolivarianism in South America is accumulating value by extracting hydrocarbons—oil and gas—and building infrastructure on contested lands. There is significant opposition to this process from indigenous peoples in Venezuela and Bolivia. As discussed earlier, the resulting wealth has been used to reduce poverty and increase education and access to health care. But when one considers these activities in the larger context of *extractivism*, this approach to development could ultimately be the basis of a new form of capitalism. And it will likely contribute to the degradation of the environment and the marginalization of some of the peoples who traditionally have used these lands.

For these reasons extractive investments and BITS contracts have been the target of peoples' movements around the world. Coalitions have been active to prevent dams and other land grabs in India, Brazil, Mexico, Haiti, Venezuela, Bolivia, and South Africa, to name a few. To be fully effective, these movements would need to be placed in the context of resistance to another global reorganization of capitalism—this would keep them from being isolated struggles against a particular land grab or dam. However, broad-based resistance could indeed close off this particular avenue to capitalist reorganization. The question always remains though, of what such movements would like to see instead of *extractivism* or any sort of capitalism.

4. Prospects for a Revolutionary Global Shift

Up to this point I have outlined three kinds of prospects for the future of capitalism. First, we could well have many more years of "churning and flailing" during which the U.S. maintains its dominance of the present system. A major point of this book, however, is that the need for capitalism to generate value, which allows the system to reproduce itself and its workers is not being met by the New World Order. Something has got to give. A long period of churning and flailing in the U.S. will include constant bickering between Republicans and Democrats, conservatives and liberals, over who can preside more effectively and which tools will better manage the failing system. A lengthy period of churning and flailing under the present circumstances is also likely to include a "permanent" fiscal crisis, further environmental degradation and the rise of a more "permanent" national security state with all of its spying, and outbreaks of secret and not so secret dirty wars around the world.

Secondly, while all that is going on, there will likely be ongoing efforts by other nations or blocs of nations to wrest control of global capitalism from the U.S., which will include attacks on the status of the dollar as the global reserve currency. The loss of the dollar's status as global reserve currency will likely make the system unworkable for many people in the U.S. and deepen the crisis of the new world disorder. If other nations are successful in taking the reins of this failing system, the present global crisis will still continue and the condition of people around the world will further deteriorate.

Thirdly, out of all the churning and flailing, a newer New World Order could emerge. In this regard, what is visible on the horizon is a kind of "primitive accumulation"—to use Adam Smith and Karl Marx's term—based largely on land grabs and the extraction of other natural resources, which have already driven millions of people into deeper poverty and accelerated environmental deterioration. If all these prospects cause you to shake your head in dismay, you are not alone. For the past five years or so there have been persistent uprisings to directly confront the impacts of churning and flailing on ordinary people like you and me. So now it's time to turn to the prospects of a revolutionary global shift that can break through the current impasse and result in radical social change.

In my introduction I stated that this is a time of great opportunity for the creation of a world in which "the full and free development of every human being is its ruling principle." But I asserted that it is also a time of great peril. I asked you to put aside all the "permanent" features of our present world by shedding the "mind-forged manacles" that limit thought, and hence, what is possible. The New World Order system has indeed enriched the few at the expense of the many and the many aren't happy about it. The slogan of the Occupy movements—we are the 99%— resonated with people all over the world, even those who did not participate in demonstrations or street battles during and in the wake of the so-called "Arab Spring."

There are lessons to be learned from the movements during the past few years in Egypt, Tunisia, Libya, Syria, Greece, Spain, the

U.S., and many other places around the world. One is that even in the most repressive regimes, insurrections can break out and expand into civil war. Places that are very quiet and seemingly complacent can suddenly explode with revolutionary fervor. But there is another lesson as well. Insurrection is not the same thing as revolution, even if the insurrection leads to the overthrow of a regime. Such an insurrection can end up simply creating a newer New World Order based on primitive accumulation. It can result in a form of state capitalism, which was what happened in the aftermath of the 1917 Russian Revolution. It can result in ongoing conflict and even civil war, which is the current situation in Egypt (conflict) and Syria (war). Or it can simply peter out without causing any real change at all, like the U.S. Occupy movements. My point is that insurrection does not make a true revolution if what happens after is left unresolved. Revolution must necessarily result in ongoing human development in which mind-forged manacles are shed and humanity can evolve. A shift of power means little without a shift in thinking, the development of a "new human being" and a new set of "impermanent permanencies." I will elaborate on that awkward notion, but first I want to describe two kinds of possible revolutionary developments.

This is not any sort of prediction or forecast; both kinds are present right now in a very nascent form. My purpose is to offer first a warning and then conclude with a description of a world in which, to use Marx's phrase, its purpose is the "full and free development of every human being."

a. The Prospects of a New Fascism

Liberals, and even revolutionary leftists, have a tendency to label any sort of government sponsored brutal, thuggish or oppressive behavior as "fascist." This is not what I mean by this term. As I discuss the "Prospects for a New Fascism," I will be using the term in a very specific way. Before going further, it is important to note that there are hundreds of books on fascism. The Amazon Kindle bookstore alone lists about 750 titles. I make no effort to review the various descriptions and debates on the subject. Rather, I supply a definition of the term that is grounded in history and useful in assessing the possibilities and consequences of a successful fascist movement today. For those of you who want to study the subject and decide for yourself whether my definition makes sense, I suggest three sources. First, is a good summary of the history and an overview of concepts in Wikipedia. (www.en.wikipedia.org/wiki/Fascism) This article has a good bibliography as well. Secondly, Leon Trotsky wrote a series of essays between 1930 and 1934 about the dangers of the fascist movement in Germany, in which he criticized the weak position being taken by Stalin and the communist international movement at that time. (www.marxists.org/archive/trotsky/works/1944/1944-fas.html) Finally, I found much insight in an essay by Don Hamerquist addressed to leftist revolutionaries who oppose fascist movements today: (www.kersplebedeb.com/mystuff/books/fascism/fashantifash.php).

Historically, there are a number of characteristics common to fascist movements and societies. For the purposes of this discussion, I have placed the "prospects for a new fascism" under the broader heading of a "revolutionary global shift." This implies that such a new fascism could become a replacement for capitalism, but it could also evolve into a new form of capitalism, vying for global power with other forms of a newer New World Order such as *extractivism*. In fact, *extractivism* itself could be combined with fascism.

A fascist society has its roots in a mass popular revolutionary movement that aims to overthrow the prevailing political and economic system and replace it with something new. The term has its roots in Italy at the turn of the 20th century. A fascist movement and system first came to power when Benito Mussolini broke with socialism and seized control of Italy in 1919. His organization called itself the Fascist Revolutionary Action Party. Similar ideas were developing in Germany around the same time that proponents called National Socialism. They formed Hitler's Nazi Party and came to power in 1933. A third fascist movement rose in Spain under the leadership of Francisco Franco who led the overthrow of the existing Spanish republic in 1936. While Hitler and Mussolini's fascist states were destroyed in 1945 with the end of World War II, Franco continued to rule Spain until his death in 1975.

Fascist principles that gave rise to the mass revolutionary movements in Italy, Germany and Spain remain to this day. These principles are an inspiration for a large number of political groupings around the world, including the U.S. The Golden Dawn Party in Greece, for example, has gained considerable strength as the crisis intensifies in that nation. Many of the affiliates of al Qaeda base their activities on principles that I consider to be fascist. In the U.S., The Southern Poverty Law Center keeps track of organizations they consider to be hate groups. In 2012, they produced a map showing the locations of over 1000 such groups across every state. They classified them as: Ku Klux Klan, Neo-

David Ranney

Nazi, White Nationalist, Racist Skinhead, Christian Identity, Neo-Confederate, Black Separatist and General Hate. All of these operate on the basis of what I would call fascist principles. What are these principles?

One is the total rejection of the present system. This means that today's conservative Republicans who wish to preserve a U.S. dominated New World Order will be opposed by Fascists with as much zeal as they oppose liberal Democrats. For this reason, right wing and conservative labels are not useful in understanding a fascist movement.

Fascism is, by definition, initiated as a mass popular movement. The masses are composed of a number of different classes of people. The middle classes who feel betrayed by the existing order have historically been key players in fascist movements. They include small business owners, workers involved in the distribution of goods and services and professional people. Another grouping would include people who have been marginalized by the system and are without a place in the social order. The long-term unemployed, returning military veterans who have been discarded by society, and gang members who live through criminal activity are examples. Historically, the military/security establishment and the owners of big capital, including finance, have joined the mass movement. But fascism needs to be understood as a mass movement and not simply the overthrow of a government by the military or a few potential dictators.

One of the things that is common to all fascist organizations and movements is that they unify around a notion that they constitute a "superior people" who desire to establish a "living space," as Hitler put it, where they can flourish without being dragged down by "inferior peoples." The superior people can be defined in many ways—race, gender, nation, religion, or some combination. Historically, the notion of a living space has always had a national dimension. This does not necessarily refer to existing national borders. Germany defined its "living space" in terms of a "Greater German" empire consisting of nations that its leaders considered to be part of an historic homeland. Greater Germany was a territory where the dominant language was German and consisted of an eclectic mix of territories that had been lost in World War I, as well as others that had acquired their German status by conquests and migrations in the distant past. Toward this end Hitler's conquests of World War II incorporated what is today the Czech Republic, Austria and parts of Poland into Germany, treating them differently from other conquests, like France, which he did not consider to be part of a Greater Germany. The broader point is that a fascist movement and society defines its living space in a way that excludes or oppresses peoples residing in their space who are considered to be "inferior."

Another common characteristic of fascism historically and of groups today that have a fascist orientation is that they mobilize around some imagined glorious past enjoyed by their particular superior people. They look to a mythologized and glorified past for inspiration and to set the goals of their movement. Hitler, for example, envisioned an ideal and actually mythical race of "Aryans" who dominated the Greater Germany of the past but had been degraded by Jews, communists, homosexuals, and Gypsies.

In order to establish a "living space" where the "special people" can flourish without the degrading influence of "inferior peoples," there must be order and discipline. So fascists rally around and support a powerful leader. Democracy is seen as weakness; it dilutes the potential of the fascist ideal. Therefore fascist societies are by definition dictatorships.

Fascists believe in the use of violence to achieve their aims. Historically, when they have achieved power they have used militarism, political police and repression to maintain order in the society. They have also used the military/security state apparatus to attack outside forces that threaten the movement or that take land they believe is theirs by historical if not God-given right.

Fascism is thus a mass movement mobilized by the idea of restoring some mythical past where a superior people could flourish in some defined territory through the agency of military/police force and the discipline and order imposed by a great leader/dictator. These principles have not only been common to fascist movements and nations in the past, they motivate groups today that aspire to the establishment of fascist societies. Since they are revolutionary and seek some form of state power or control over their "living spaces," a question remains about what a "fascist society" might look like. What would be the nature of its economy and social system?

Historically, fascism has been a form of capitalism. In an earlier section I argued that, "what makes capitalism *capitalism* is the process of creating and distributing value." The measure of value in any capitalist system is the amount of labor time required to produce the goods and services needed to reproduce society and its labor force. Further, "The secret of a capitalist system is

221

that workers produce more value than they get in return for their labor time." In these terms, fascism has always been capitalist. In the case of Germany, Italy and Spain in the first half of the 20th Century, the owners of capital united with the fascist movement and the new fascist government. One writer stated that it was capitalism at its worst: raw state power combined with a brutal form of capitalism. It was an economic and political unification of capital. (Based on Gilles Dauve (2004), *When Insurrections Die.* Translated by Loren Goldner (1999), Antagonism Press.) But as I noted earlier, a fascist system could abolish the institution of wage labor and establish something altogether different.

Today's crisis is a toxic stew that leaves society susceptible to fascist movements. That stew includes: paralysis of both capitalist private enterprise and governments; the inability of the new world disorder to generate enough value to keep the global system going; and an inability of the system to even sustain the people who live in it. These elements could breed a fascist movement capable of overthrowing and replacing the new world disorder. Increasingly, there are masses of unemployed and disaffected peoples around the world who will find considerable appeal in finding their identity as a part of a "special people" who need "living space," and a life grounded in some glorious if mythical past.

Such is the particular logic of secessionist movements, where the people of a particular region attempt to separate from the larger nation. There are active secessionist movements in Northern Italy, the Catalonia region in Spain, as well as in Scotland and Texas. The Texas Aryan Brotherhood is clearly fascist as I have defined it. The same is true of the so-called U.S. "hate groups" identified by the Southern Poverty Law Center. In addition, there are a multitude of individuals who identify with conservative groups, such as many in the "Tea Party movement," who have given up on the Republican Party and could begin to find a more revolutionary path of a fascist nature.

Currently, the various hate groups and alienated individuals in the U.S. lack a coherent enough outlook to mobilize into a single mass fascist popular movement. But some of the elements are already in place. Any revolutionary popular movement would have to be built on a mix of today's common sense and an attack on those elements of common sense that contradict the actual life of masses of people. Think back to the historic principles of fascism I outlined earlier. The mobilization of a mass fascist popular movement would require a "special people" narrative that either specifically contradicted or was reinforced by elements of common sense. This "special people" notion could be built upon the idea of American Exceptionalism discussed earlier. The ideal of "America" is that we are an exceptional people who do what we do in the world and at home for a greater good. It is a short step from exceptional to special and superior. Thus this concept could be a building block, further refined by the exclusion of some residents of America who for one reason or another are not really "American."

Many of the groupings listed by the Southern Poverty Law Center as "hate groups" that have fascist leanings base their "special people" claims on Christian identity. I am not contending that all who have a distinct Christian identity have fascist leanings, but the ideology of what we now call the "Christian Right" in the U.S. could ultimately be a base for a fascist movement. Right now masses of people in the U.S. consider it a nation "under God." That could narrow the definition of who is considered American and who is not.

Then there is the matter of race. The U.S., founded on the institution of slavery and genocide against its native peoples, has a historic context for exclusion of peoples based in part on a racialized definition of being American. Historian Noel Ignatiev has written extensively on this subject (*How the Irish Became White* (2012), and, with John Garvey, *Race Traitor* (1996)). Ignatiev argues convincingly that race is not a biological condition but rather an assigned social category. In the U.S. this has been primarily based on skin color. Social and economic advantages have been bestowed on those defined as "white." The Irish were not considered "white" when they initially came to the U.S. but received this status once they engaged in anti-Black violence as their path of entry into "white" society. There is, therefore, a long history of defining people based on not just skin color but on some "racial" construction of what it means to be an "American." Today, skin color, immigration status, national origin and religion are ready made categories that could be used by a mass movement to define who is a part of the special people/ exceptional club and who is not.

There are also a number of "cultural issues" today that could help mobilize a fascist movement in the United States. Religion is a large and important category in this regard. This is especially true when religion is mixed with attitudes toward homosexuality, the role of women in society, and a women's right to choose whether or not to give birth. Historically, such matters have been part of fascism in Europe and they could once again play a role in a fascist movement in the U.S.

Social class is an important element with regard to prospects for a new fascism. As the New World Order descends into a new world disorder, many people in the U.S. and other nations who identified themselves as "middle class" (by which they meant middle income) are finding their status under attack. This began with the destruction of manufacturing jobs that paid living wages in what were once "industrialized nations." Workers who once could afford a home and a decent car, who had health care benefits through the job, and could afford to send their kids to college or get them a decent paying job through their unions have seen that situation evaporate. When the New World Order offered them and their children the opportunity to maintain or extend their "middle class" lifestyle through easy credit, they jumped at the chance and sunk deeper in debt. Then began the period of crisis that included the collapse of derivative markets and a subsequent tightening of credit. Those who were the "middle class on credit" once again saw their situation deteriorate—some were even evicted from their homes. The new world disorder has also driven some into poverty while others have been left completely out of the mix. Their anger is now a key factor in American and European politics, and it could be an entry point into a new fascist movement. Today that anger often takes the form of being anti-government—tea party politics. Tomorrow it could turn against the system.

There is a lot more to say about the prospects for fascism in other parts of the world. Dynamics similar to those discussed above are occurring in Europe, the Middle East, Asia and Africa. Whether the global intifada, including potential rebellion in the U.S., gets played out as a new fascism or as some anti-capitalist and anti-fascist alternative is yet to be determined. So what could a revolutionary alternative to fascism look like?

b. An Alternative to Fascism: A Personal Statement

There are many revolutionary alternatives to a new form of fascism. I am going to conclude with what I consider is a more hopeful note by describing one of them. I'll also include some brief notes on how a movement might move in a direction consistent with such an alternative. My point of view has been developed over many years of participation in movement activity and has been inspired by a large number of revolutionary thinkers, writers and friends. In describing this alternative, I hesitate to use labels like "right" and "left," or even "socialism." These words have a variety of meanings to those who use them based on their own reading and experience. I don't think they have any universal meaning anymore, so I'll start with a more generic formulation developed by Don Hamerquist in his essay on fascism. He is discussing the spontaneous anti-fascist activities of what he calls

> "rebellious and anti-authoritarian young people (who have a) gut level rejection of traditional fascist notions: who's superior and who's inferior, what constitutes a good life and what's corrupt."

He goes on to elaborate on the differences he sees between fascists and these anti-fascist youth:

> "Fascists want a society and culture restricted to those they define as superior people. We don't. They want discipline and order; we want autonomy and creativity. Their goal is an idealized, basically mythical past; we want a totally different future. They line up behind

226

maximum leaders; we want a critical and conscious rank and file."

A movement that aims to build a revolutionary alternative to both fascism and all the other prospects I have just discussed needs to address the following questions: What are goals of a new society that are neither fascist nor capitalist? How can such a vision address and connect to the anger of masses of people who are ready to reject today's new world disorder? What are some concrete elements of a new society?

Let's start with some goals, or a vision of alternatives, to both capitalism and fascism. My own ideas are inspired by Marx's formulation of a "society in which the full and free development of every human being is its ruling principle." This formulation has within it a basic sense of both equality and what constitutes fairness. It is not only a challenge to the fascist notion of special or superior people; it is contradictory to capitalism as well. As formulated earlier, the basis of any sort of capitalist society is not the full and free development of every human being. Instead, the most basic goal of a capitalist society is greater production (economic growth) that can yield value with enough surplus to enrich the owners of capital and enable them to reproduce the system. There also must be enough value production to enable the producers of value to reproduce themselves. For this reason, capitalism has been described as a system of production for the sake of production. This book has demonstrated why this ruling principle of capitalism leads to crisis and environmental degradation.

But even in the best of times, production for the sake of production tends to undermine the "full and free development of every human being." In a capitalist system human development must serve production. By necessity, all work must be performed in such a manner that workers produce the most possible in the shortest period of time. Economists call that productivity. Higher wages are necessarily tied to higher productivity because wages are a share of value production. If total value production is a big pie, the worker's piece will not get bigger unless the owner of the pie reduces his share or the pie itself gets bigger. Since the owner needs to maintain his/her share to keep the whole system going, the bigger pie must come from increased productivity. In a capitalist system, education, job training, and investment in machines are driven by the need to raise productivity rather than the quality of life of the workers. Labor in such a system has one function: to produce as much value possible in the shortest period of time, and that negates its function as a meaningful and creative process that enhances the development of the worker. And if workers get "too much" of the value they produce, if they fail to produce a sufficient surplus of value, the system goes into crisis mode and their claims on the value they produce are destroyed, one way or another.

However, it is possible to envision a different sort of society, where production serves the goal of human development, where labor is a part of life, and where wealth or value is measured in terms of quality of life of all the people who make up society. Marx's formulation of wealth is instructive:

> "...what is wealth if not the universality of the individual's needs, capacities, enjoyments, productive forces, etc. produced in universal exchange; what is it if not the full development of human control over the forces of nature—over the forces of so-called Nature, as

David Ranney

well as those of his own nature? What is wealth if not the absolute unfolding of man's creative abilities, without any precondition other than the preceding historical development, which makes the totality of this development—i.e. the development of all human powers as such, not measured by any previously given yardstick—an end-in-itself, through which he does not reproduce himself in any determined form, but produces his totality? Where he does not seek to remain something formed by the past but is in an absolute movement of becoming?" (Karl Marx "Outlines of the Critique of Political Economy (Grundrisse)," *Collected Works*, vol. 28, New York: International Publishers, 1986 p. 411-12)

Wealth or value in this vision is not measured by labor time or money. Rather the measure of wealth includes the "needs, capacities, enjoyments and creative abilities" of each person. Life itself is seen as the unhindered process of wealth creation in this sense. The key phrase is that wealth creation through labor is an "absolute movement of becoming" meaning self-development.

How far this vision is from fascism with its special/superior people, its exaltation of some mythical past, its exaltation of some great "leader" who is to be a dictator, its placement of order and discipline over individual creativity and freedom! How far this vision is from the so-called "worker states" of the Soviet Union and China that in fact preserved a system of production for the sake of production under the control of brutal dictatorships! And how far this is from the present system where the owners of capital will do anything to squeeze more surplus value out of workers and appropriate it to reproduce the system and enrich themselves!

They have closed factories in the U.S. and Europe where workers struggled for enough value to reproduce themselves, moving production into fire traps in less developed countries where child labor and young women can be super exploited. How far is this vision of a new society from a society that creates phantom products to sell in phantom markets, throwing workers into a state of homelessness once the fictions of the debt commodity and the markets they exchange in are exposed! How far is this alternative vision of a society in which nature serves the needs of human development, from the present system in which nature is forced to serve the needs of production to the point of humanity's possible extinction! How far this vision is from the present system that needs perpetual war, the murder of innocent people with drone strikes, and national security states to protect itself from a world in rebellion!

Some may object that this vision runs against "human nature." But human nature is not a biological and permanent condition. Marx argued that human development is a process of gaining human control over "our own nature." So the process of revolution can and must involve gaining control of our nature. Revolution must involve the creation of a new human being whose nature is not shaped by the past, but fully supports and brings into being an alternative vision of a new society. Revolution cannot be limited to the overthrow of the social order but must simultaneously begin the process of throwing off the "mind-forged manacles" that keep human nature within the bounds of a capitalistic society. Bringing human nature into line with the sort of new society broadly outlined above is also critical to combatting the fascist ideas that are waiting in the wings.

At the heart of this alternative vision of a new society is the goal that the full and free development of every human being can bring about a society in which the needs, capacities and enjoyment of all is the true definition of wealth—the point of society. Furthermore, society and its associated human nature cannot be bound by the capitalist law of value, where production rather than human development is the goal. There are historical examples where crisis and revolt unleashed possibilities lying dormant in ordinary people who had been mired in the notion that their present condition was permanent. These examples go back to the origins of capitalism, and include not only periods of revolution but day-to-day struggles in workplaces and communities. Here are just a few examples that have shaped my own thinking.

In 1871, an uprising in Paris resulted in the establishment of an entire new system known as the Paris Commune. It lasted just a few months until the military crushed it after a brutal assault. But while in power, the Communards, who had been living under both monarchies and capitalistic republics, established a government run by councils of elected delegates, with recall provisions, from all sectors of Paris society. They established councils of workers to run businesses. They developed councils of women to pursue an agenda of gender equality. They postponed paying of debts and eliminated interest rates. They took measures to separate church and state, as the church at this time was a major player in government oppression. They did away with night work for bakers and radically altered many more aspects of daily life that inhibited human development, and were roadblocks to meeting the needs of the populace. I am not trying to develop a model of any sort in presenting this, but I do want to give an example of how people, under the most stressful and dire conditions, can find alternatives that meet long and short term needs using their vision and desire for freedom and self-development as a guide.

In the course of my own experience I have seen this ability in an admittedly embryonic state. Between 1977 and 1981 I did factory work. In 1979, there was a wildcat strike against both company and union at a factory where I worked. Workers showed an amazing capacity for self-organization that included scheduling pickets, holding democratic meetings to decide on tactics, organizing mutual assistance activities and food sharing. In an atmosphere of prior racial antagonism, the solidarity they developed gave me a glimpse of the possibilities of multicultural living and governance. During the course of the strike, we had the opportunity to discuss the possibility that their aspirations could become reality. I witnessed concretely that these working people had within them the seeds of a new society. I experienced other less dramatic examples as well, and have seen the seeds of a new society in both the workplace and community. There are thousands of examples like this that demonstrate that the basis for a new society such as I have described is deeply embedded in all of us. But also embedded is the "human nature" of the present society that most people see as permanent. And there are aspects of human consciousness that could be open to a fascist order as well.

We can also point to examples of failed or unfinished revolutions, and of counter-revolution. Like the Paris Commune, some revolutions have been crushed, as have many movements that have not achieved an actual overthrow. The Russian Revolution of 1917 began with a vision of a society run by and for its own people. Soviets were to be councils that were run by democratically elected ordinary people. That never happened. Ultimately, when some of the soviets attempted to operate against the wishes of the Communist Party they were crushed, and the so-called "Soviet" Union descended into a dictatorial form of state capitalism. At the present time, the various uprisings known as the Arab Spring have failed to develop an alternative to the systems the people were living under. As I write the regimes that replaced dictators in Egypt, Libya and Tunisia have not met the aspirations of the masses of people who overthrew the former rulers. But the struggle continues. In the U.S. the wave of protests known as Occupy continue to be just protests and have accomplished little.

I don't have a cookbook or manual on how to turn a movement into the sort of revolution that I think is needed. But I do have a few thoughts on the subject. First of all, every revolutionary movement needs to have what writer Raya Dunayevskaya called a "dual rhythm." Briefly, that rhythm includes a collective understanding and agreement on what the movement is against and then a similar coming together on what it is for. Masses of people mobilize initially with a common desire to get rid of whatever stands in the way of full human development. This could involve a strike against a company, a protest against a war, or an even broader protest against an unfair system that enriches some and impoverishes many, such as the Arab Spring and Occupy movements. But the act of resistance itself opens up possibilities that go beyond the bounds of what is considered practical or permanent. This does not happen automatically or spontaneously. Many a movement has fallen short because it has failed to address the question of what it is for.

What sort of society are we seeking? Unless there is a conscious effort to give voice and form to the revolutionary ideas implied by the acts of rebellion, the movement will either fall short of its potential or it will end in failure, co-optation by the present system, or descent into fascism and barbarism.

From my own experience in movement activity there is nearly always a tendency to put aside the difficult discussions of "what we are for" in favor of immediate tactical considerations— where and when will the next demonstration be, what sort of tactics will we use etc.? Those questions are, of course, very important. But confining ourselves to the nuts and bolts of activism will cause the movement itself to ultimately flounder and subject itself to co-optation or fail to go beyond the immediate issues. Limiting movement activity to the practical, achievable, winnable issues mutes the voices that can bring a broader vision to life.

This is where a different kind of leadership can make a difference. It is fashionable these days to downgrade leadership and to create models of "horizontal decision making." It is possible to have a protest and possibly to overthrow a regime without much leadership, but it is not possible to have a revolution that fully opens up visions for a new kind of society without leadership. Also, it is wrong to confuse leadership with dictatorship. Leadership in a revolutionary situation must first and foremost be accountable. That is what the communards attempted to accomplish in Paris by establishing councils of delegates with clear recall provisions. Leadership also needs to be geared to giving voice to the highest ideals of those who have been oppressed; to find in ordinary people the seeds of a new society rather than imposing some preconceived idea hammered out by a political party or small group rump session. But leadership must also address the aspirations of people with some distinct challenges to both capitalism and fascism.

A revolutionary movement must challenge the most basic element of capitalism, which is that value is measured in money terms by prices and generated by labor time and that wealth is accumulated money, property and things. In Thomas Paine's time, the common sense ideal that *everyone* has the right to life, liberty and the pursuit of happiness was contradicted by the subservience of the people to the king. Today life, liberty and pursuit of happiness are contradicted by the operations of the law of value. The insatiable appetite of the new world disorder for human-produced value undermines the basic needs of most people in the world. Australian thinker and activist Anitra Nelson and Dutch diplomat Frans Timmerman argue that:

> "...dispensing with the market is a key and necessary strategy to achieve socialism, not simply a state that we will reach once the appropriate political or economic structures are in place or people's consciousness has become sufficiently socialist." (Anitra Nelson and Frans Timmerman, *Life Without Money: Building Fair and Sustainable Economies,* Pluto Press, 2011.)

In short, moving beyond capitalism requires the abolition of the law of value and money in its present form.

Any sort of fascism where the human development of special and superior people is placed above others, where some people are excluded from society altogether, and where each individual must bend to the will of a law-and-order-enforcing dictator, is also contradictory to the notion of the free and full development of *every* human being. In the U.S. context, the idea of American

Exceptionalism that is used to justify foreign policy also runs counter to these same ideals. Multiculturalism and internationalism can be presented as ideals more in line with the sense of fairness and equality that is an essential element of the revolutionary vision I have presented here.

The basic problem for leadership of a revolutionary movement that aspires to such a vision is that both sides of the contradictions between capitalism or fascism, and the sort of society I envision, are present in most of us. Most feel that the law of value, and the institutions of our government and how they operate are permanent—moving outside this "permanency" would be impractical if not downright scary. Also, many people in the U.S. fear a world that rejects American Exeptionalism and one where America is not "the most powerful nation in the world." At the same time, the ideals of a very different sort of world are part of our consciousness as well.

The contradictions in our own worldview become apparent in the course of a struggle, which raises an opportunity for discussions about what the movement is for. I believe that the vision I have laid out here in general terms can be made concrete in the aspirations of people in actual revolt. For example, in Chicago and many other cities in the U.S., there is a vibrant movement to oppose foreclosures and evictions. Some of those about to be evicted or who have been evicted face homelessness. Once they join the movement and attempt to block other evictions they are, through their actions, raising a broader question that is a challenge to capitalism itself: *What is a home in our society?* For ordinary people, a home is a place where you can be protected from the elements, raise a family and enjoy simple pleasures. But the government and the banks consider it to be primarily a commodity to be bought and sold and, through the medium of money, exchanged for other commodities. For most people, banks legally own the house they consider their home. If the residents can't make their mortgage payments, the human concept of home gets pushed to the background and they are evicted and may become homeless. Blocking an eviction or occupying one of these houses and turning it into a home is an act of disputing the primacy of house over home. The leadership of such anti-eviction activity has a role to play in bringing to the surface what is implicit in the actions of eviction resisters. And a discussion of house and home raises possibilities for a very different kind of society. If, on the other hand, anti-eviction work gets reduced to legal battles in the courts and the logistics of getting resisters to a particular site, the opportunity to raise the broader question of home vs. house and the possibility of a new society are lost.

I believe that in the midst of today's global intifada there is the potential to raise the issue of what sort of world we want to live in. Notions of permanency and practicality are part and parcel of the existing system. But permanency is always impermanent. Our task is to find the contradictions in the prevailing common sense and help bring about a new society built on a totally new foundation.

This book is an effort to explain the nature of our world today so that as the new world disorder sinks deeper into crisis and the global intifada spreads, we can all participate in an effort to find the seeds of a new society in the hearts and minds of all of us. I hope these reflections at a time of great opportunity and great peril will contribute to forming a better world.

Discussion Questions

1. What are the consequences and prospects for an extended period of churning and flailing? Do you believe the present system can be made to work?

2. Discuss the prospects for the U.S. being able to hold onto its leadership role in global capitalism?

3. What is the meaning and significance of the dollar's status as a global reserve currency?

4. What are some examples of what the author termed "extractivism?" Do you believe such practices could be a basis for a reorganized capitalist system? What would the implications of such a development be for those living in the U.S. and Europe?

5. What is the popular appeal of fascism as the author defines it?

6. Do you know of any groups or political parties today that are or have the potential to be fascist?

7. Do you believe that the vision of a new society described by the author could be the basis for a political movement as an alternative to both capitalism and fascism? Why or why not?

Glossary of Terms

Assessed Value: The value assigned to real estate by governments as a basis for property taxation.

Capitalism: A political economic system in which workers create value through their labor and receive less value for their labor than they create.

Carrying Capacity: The amount of pollution and waste that can be cleaned up and processed on the earth without a build-up of pollution.

Counterinsurgency: A military strategy aimed at building new societies that would be part of the New World Order, which is capable of keeping out terrorists and other forces opposed to the global order.

Counterterrorism: A military strategy aimed at destroying stateless terror groups like al Qaeda.

Crisis of Value: A global political and economic crisis that occurs when the claims on the value generated by the global capitalist system are greater than the system is capable of producing.

Derivative: A piece of paper that has a price derived from the price of some underlying asset.

Ecological Economics: A branch of economics that places limits on sustainable economic growth rates that are defined by the *carrying capacity* of the *ecosystem*.

Ecosystem: An area including the Earth and the atmosphere that surrounds it that enables us to take solar energy from the sun and create what we need to live on Earth.

Environmental Degradation: That which occurs when economic growth and development exceed the *ecosystem's carrying capacity*.

Exchange Value: The price of any commodity at any particular time.

Extractivism: A form of capitalism in which the main engine for the accumulation of value is the extraction of natural resources including minerals, water, forests, and land.

Fascism: A mass movement mobilized by the idea of restoring some mythical or ideal past where a "superior people" could flourish in some defined territory through the use of military force and the discipline imposed by a dictator.

Hedge Funds: A highly speculative private investment fund consisting of stocks, bonds, real estate and other financial assets that charges a performance fee based on the returns its members receive on their investment in the hedge fund.

Labor Theory of Value: The basis for value in a capitalist system is the necessary labor time needed to produce goods and needed services.

Maquiladora: A zone in Mexico where goods are produced for export. The more general term is "export processing zones," which are located all over the world.

Phantom Markets: Capitalist markets where goods and services without value (based on labor time) are traded.

Precautionary Principle: A basis for environmental standards or regulations that suggests that if there is any reason to suspect something might be harmful to the environment or human health, it is not allowed.

Price: The exchange value of a good or service at a particular time.

Real Income: The purchasing power of income that is usually measured in terms of the relationship of income to prices.

Socialism: A political economic system that devotes the fruits of labor to meeting the needs of all while seeking the full contribution from all people based on their ability.

State Capitalism: A capitalist political economic system where government owns and runs all or most economic enterprise.

Traunch: A group of mortgages with similar characteristics within a bond made up of mortgages with different characteristics.

Use Value: The value attached to a good or service based on its usefulness to those who need it.

References

Bond, Patrick. *BRICS in Africa: Anti Imperialist, Sub Imperialist, or in Between?* www.ukzn.ac.za/files/bond ccs booklet 22 March 2013.pdf

Daly, Herman and Joshua Farley. *Ecological Economics*, Island Press, 2005.

Dauve, Gilles. *When Insurrections Fail*. Tr. By Loren Goldner, Antagonism Press, 1999.

Dunayevskaya, Raya. *Philosophy and Revolution: From Hegel to Sartre and from Marx to Mao*, Delta Press, 1973.

Eichengreen, Barry. *Exorbitant Privilege: The Rise and Fall of the Dollar and the Future of the International Monetary System*, Oxford University Press, 2010.

Fairbairn, Madeleine. " 'Like gold with yield:' Evolving intersections between farmland and finance," in *Food Sovereignty: A Critical Dialogue*, International Conference, Conference Paper No. 6, Yale University, September 14-15, 2013.

Fukuyama, Francis. *America at the Crossroads*, Yale University Press, 2006.

Goldner, Loren. *The Remaking of the Working Class: The Restructuring of Global Capital and the The Recomposition of Class Terrain*, 1991. www.home.earthlink.net/lgoldner

Gramsci, Antonio. "Philosophy, Common Sense, Language and Folklore," in David Forcacs, *An Antonio Gramsci Reader, Selected Writings (1916-35)*, Schoctin Press, 1988, pp. 323-62.

Hammerquist, Don. *Fascism and Anti-Fascism,* www.kersplebedeb.com/mystuff/books/fascisms/fashantifash.php.

Harvey, David. *A Brief History of Neoliberalism,* Oxford University Press, 2007.

Harvey, David. *The New Imperialism,* Oxford University Press, 2003.

Ignatiev, Noel. *How the Irish Became White,* Routledge, 1995.

Jaques, Martin. *When China Rules the World: The End of the Western World and the Birth of a New Global Order,* Penguin Press, 2009.

Kaufman, Frederick. "The Food Bubble: How Wall Street Starved Millions and Got Away With It," *Harpers Magazine,* July 2010, pp. 27-33.

Kristol, Irving. *Neo-Conservativism: The Autobiography of an Idea,* Simon and Schuster, 1995.

Lewis, Michael. *The Big Short: Inside the Doomsday Machine,* W.W. Norton, 2010.

McKibben, William. *Eaarth,* Henry Holt, 2010.

Marx, Karl. "Outlines of the Critique of Political Economy," *Collected Works,* v. 28, International Publishers, 1986.

Mattick, Paul. *Business as Usual,* Reaktion Books, 2011.

Mazzetti, Mark. *The Way of The Knife: The CIA, The Secret Army, and a War at the Ends of the Earth,* Penguin Press, 2013.

Nelson, Anitra and Frans Timmerman, *Life Without Money: Building Fair and Sustainable Communities,* Pluto Press, 2011.

O'Connor, Alice. *Poverty Knowledge,* Princeton University Press, 2001.

Ranney, David C. *Global Decisions, Local Collisions: Urban Life in the New World Order,* Temple University Press, 2003.

Scahill, Jeremy. *Dirty Wars: The World as a Battlefield,* Nation Books, 2013.

Suppan, Steve. *Excessive Speculation in Agricultural Commodities: Selections from 2008-11,* Institute for Agriculture and Trade Policy, www.iatp.org

Wood, Helen Meiksins. *Empires of Capital,* Verso Press, 2003.

Woodward, Bob, *Obama's Wars,* Simon and Schuster, 2010.

Wright, Lawrence. *The Looming Tower: Al Qaeda and the Road to 9/11.* Alfred A. Knopf, 2006.